THINK
THIS

101 BREAKTHROUGH THOUGHTS FOR A BREAKTHROUGH LIFE

NOT
THAT

JOEL OSTEEN MINISTRIES

Think This Not That

Copyright © 2023 Joel Osteen

Printed in USA

ISBN: 978-1-951701-44-4

Created and assembled for Joel Osteen Ministries by
Breakfast for Seven
2150 E. Continental Blvd., Southlake, TX 76092
breakfastforseven.com

For additional resources by Joel Osteen, visit JoelOsteen.com

You have the ability to set your life in a whole new direction. Favor, strength, confidence, health, joy, new opportunities, contentment — it all begins with one thing . . . your thoughts.

The thoughts you think determine the life that you are going to live. The Scripture says it this way: *"For as he thinks in his heart, so is he . . . "* (Proverbs 23:7). That means your thoughts are fundamental in the outcome of your day, your week, your year and the future ahead of you.

If you meditate on negative, bitter, hopeless thoughts, you're going to set your life in a negative direction. However, if you choose to think positive, faith-filled, hope-filled thoughts, you'll be amazed at what God can do in this next season of your life.

In the pages of this book, we've identified negative thoughts to avoid. The thoughts that tell us, *I'm not qualified. I don't have what it takes. Things are never going to be better. My best days are behind me* — these are thoughts that try to bring us down. But we don't have to accept these thoughts. We can choose something different.

With each negative thought to avoid, I've listed a promise-filled truth from Scripture for you to embrace — thoughts that remind you who you are in Christ Jesus and the exceeding, abundantly good plan God has for your life. It's one thing to avoid the negative, but it is even more important to meditate on God's promises . . . to think *this*, not that.

In order to see the dream God has placed in your heart come true, I encourage you to take captive the thoughts that are playing in your mind and have held you back. You can't control what others say or what your situation looks like, but you can control how you think about it. You can choose to trust God's Word and His plan for your life.

As you read the positive, hope-filled, faith-building thoughts in this book, I encourage you to make them your own. Meditate on them throughout the day. Turn them into declarations of God's favor, goodness, provision, protection, healing, and abundance for you and those you love. You are going to be amazed at how your life changes when you take those steps.

A shift is coming. New opportunities, bigger dreams, bolder prayers, unexpected good breaks, promotion you didn't even ask for. But it begins with your thoughts. Line up your thoughts with God's promises today, and prepare to walk into a whole new level of breakthrough. Think this, not that — it's a powerful way to live.

Joel

TABLE OF CONTENTS

1

MY FUTURE

 **THINK THIS:**

I choose to hope for good things because I know God is for me.

 NOT THAT:

This situation is hopeless.

Blessed is the man who trusts in the LORD, and whose hope is the LORD. For he shall be like a tree planted by the waters, which spreads out its roots by the river, and will not fear when heat comes; but its leaf will be green, and will not be anxious in the year of drought, nor will cease from yielding fruit.
JEREMIAH 17:7–8

There is hope in your future, says the LORD . . .
JEREMIAH 31:17

Why are you cast down, O my soul? And why are you disquieted within me? Hope in God, for I shall yet praise Him for the help of His countenance.
PSALM 42:5

For I know the thoughts that I think toward you, says the LORD, thoughts of peace and not of evil, to give you a future and a hope.
JEREMIAH 29:11

Now hope does not disappoint, because the love of God has been poured out in our hearts by the Holy Spirit Who was given to us.
ROMANS 5:5

This I recall to my mind, there I have hope. Through the LORD's mercies we are not consumed, because His compassions fail not. They are new every morning; great is Your faithfulness.
LAMENTATIONS 3:21–23

This hope we have as an anchor of the soul, both sure and steadfast, and which enters the Presence behind the veil . . .
HEBREWS 6:19

Hope in the LORD; for with the LORD there is mercy, and with Him is abundant redemption.
PSALM 130:7

 THINK THIS:
The best is yet to come.

 NOT THAT:
Things will never get better.

We also glory in tribulations, knowing that tribulation produces perseverance; and perseverance, character; and character, hope. Now hope does not disappoint, because the love of God has been poured out in our hearts by the Holy Spirit Who was given to us.
ROMANS 5:3–5

Therefore be patient, brethren, until the coming of the Lord. See how the farmer waits for the precious fruit of the earth, waiting patiently for it until it receives the early and latter rain. You also be patient. Establish your hearts, for the coming of the Lord is at hand.
JAMES 5:7-8

If we hope for what we do not see, we eagerly wait for it with perseverance.
ROMANS 8:25

In returning and rest you shall be saved; in quietness and confidence shall be your strength.
ISAIAH 30:15

. . . knowing that the testing of your faith produces patience. But let patience have its perfect work, that you may be perfect and complete, lacking nothing.
JAMES 1:3-4

Wait on the LORD; be of good courage, and He shall strengthen your heart; wait, I say, on the LORD!
PSALM 27:14

For you have need of endurance, so that after you have done the will of God, you may receive the promise.
HEBREWS 10:36

 **THINK THIS:**

My life is in God's hands; He is making a way.

 NOT THAT:

I have to look out for myself; no one else will.

Take My yoke upon you and learn from Me, for I am gentle and lowly in heart, and you will find rest for your souls.
MATTHEW 11:29

I wait for the LORD, my soul waits, and in His word do I hope.
PSALM 130:5

Let us hold fast the confession of our hope without wavering, for He Who promised is faithful.
HEBREWS 10:23

But those who wait on the LORD shall renew their strength; they shall mount up with wings like eagles, they shall run and not be weary, they shall walk and not faint.
ISAIAH 40:31

The LORD is good to those who wait for Him, to the soul who seeks Him.
LAMENTATIONS 3:25

Rest in the LORD, and wait patiently for Him; do not fret because of him who prospers in his way, because of the man who brings wicked schemes to pass. Cease from anger, and forsake wrath. Do not fret — it only causes harm. For evildoers shall be cut off; but those who wait on the LORD, they shall inherit the earth.

PSALM 37:7-9

Behold, I will do a new thing, Now it shall spring forth; Shall you not know it? I will even make a road in the wilderness and rivers in the desert.

ISAIAH 43:19

 **THINK THIS:**

My mind is healthy and at peace.

 **NOT THAT:**

There is so much to worry about that I just can't stop.

LORD, You will establish peace for us, for You have also done all our works in us.

ISAIAH 26:12

The kingdom of God is not eating and drinking, but righteousness and peace and joy in the Holy Spirit. For he who serves Christ in these things is acceptable to God and approved by men. Therefore let us pursue the things which make for peace and the things by which one may edify another.

ROMANS 14:17-19

Be anxious for nothing, but in everything by prayer and supplication, with thanksgiving, let your requests be made known to God; and the peace of God, which surpasses all understanding, will guard your hearts and minds through Christ Jesus.
PHILIPPIANS 4:6–7

Now may the God of hope fill you with all joy and peace in believing, that you may abound in hope by the power of the Holy Spirit.
ROMANS 15:13

Great peace have those who love Your law, and nothing causes them to stumble.
PSALM 119:165

Peace I leave with you, My peace I give to you; not as the world gives do I give to you. Let not your heart be troubled, neither let it be afraid.
JOHN 14:27

You will keep him in perfect peace, whose mind is stayed on You, because he trusts in You.
ISAIAH 26:3

Therefore, having been justified by faith, we have peace with God through our Lord Jesus Christ . . .
ROMANS 5:1

For you shall go out with joy, and be led out with peace; the mountains and the hills shall break forth into singing before you, and all the trees of the field shall clap their hands.

ISAIAH 55:12

I will both lie down in peace, and sleep; for You alone, O LORD, make me dwell in safety.

PSALM 4:8

 **THINK THIS:**

I'm strong, confident, healthy, and well able.

 **NOT THAT:**

I'm too old to do the things in my heart.

He shall call upon Me, and I will answer him; I will be with him in trouble; I will deliver him and honor him. With long life I will satisfy him, and show him My salvation.

PSALM 91:15–16

But those who wait on the LORD shall renew their strength; they shall mount up with wings like eagles, they shall run and not be weary, they shall walk and not faint.

ISAIAH 40:31

The righteous shall flourish like a palm tree, he shall grow like a cedar in Lebanon. Those who are planted in the house of the LORD shall flourish in the courts of our God. They shall still bear fruit

in old age; they shall be fresh and flourishing, to declare that the LORD is upright; He is my rock, and there is no unrighteousness in Him.
PSALM 92:12–15

But as for me, I trust in You, O LORD; I say, "You are my God." My times are in Your hand; deliver me from the hand of my enemies, and from those who persecute me.
PSALM 31:14–15

The fear of the LORD prolongs days, but the years of the wicked will be shortened.
PROVERBS 10:27

You shall walk in all the ways which the LORD your God has commanded you, that you may live and that it may be well with you, and that you may prolong your days in the land which you shall possess.
DEUTERONOMY 5:33

The fear of the LORD is the beginning of wisdom, and the knowledge of the Holy One is understanding. For by me your days will be multiplied, and years of life will be added to you.
PROVERBS 9:10–11

He who would love life and see good days, let him refrain his tongue from evil, and his lips from speaking deceit.
1 PETER 3:10

THINK THIS:
God can turn any situation
around for my good.

NOT THAT:
I'm afraid something bad is going to happen.

The LORD, is my strength and song; He also has
become my salvation.
ISAIAH 12:2

. . . in Whom we have boldness and access with
confidence through faith in Him.
EPHESIANS 3:12

This hope we have as an anchor of the soul, both
sure and steadfast, and which enters the Presence
behind the veil . . .
HEBREWS 6:19

There is no fear in love; but perfect love casts out
fear, because fear involves torment. But he who
fears has not been made perfect in love.
1 JOHN 4:18

For this reason I also suffer these things; nevertheless I am not ashamed, for I know Whom I have
believed and am persuaded that He is able to keep
what I have committed to Him until that Day.
2 TIMOTHY 1:12

Being confident of this very thing, that He Who has begun a good work in you will complete it until the day of Jesus Christ . . .
PHILIPPIANS 1:6

My flesh and my heart fail; but God is the strength of my heart and my portion forever.
PSALM 73:26

The work of righteousness will be peace, and the effect of righteousness, quietness and assurance forever.
ISAIAH 32:17

 *THINK THIS:*
God is my protector and defender.

 NOT THAT:
I can't handle these things that are coming against me.

But You, O LORD, are a shield for me, my glory and the One Who lifts up my head.
PSALM 3:3

The eternal God is your refuge, and underneath are the everlasting arms; He will thrust out the enemy from before you . . .
DEUTERONOMY 33:27

The LORD your God, Who goes before you, He will fight for you . . .
DEUTERONOMY 1:30

For this reason I also suffer these things; nevertheless I am not ashamed, for I know Whom I have believed and am persuaded that He is able to keep what I have committed to Him until that Day.
2 TIMOTHY 1:12

The Lord is faithful, Who will establish you and guard you from the evil one.
2 THESSALONIANS 3:3

When you pass through the waters, I will be with you; and through the rivers, they shall not overflow you. When you walk through the fire, you shall not be burned, nor shall the flame scorch you.
ISAIAH 43:2

As the mountains surround Jerusalem, so the LORD surrounds His people from this time forth and forever.
PSALM 125:2

But if you indeed obey His voice and do all that I speak, then I will be an enemy to your enemies and an adversary to your adversaries.
EXODUS 23:22

A thousand may fall at your side, and ten thousand at your right hand; but it shall not come near you.
PSALM 91:7

THINK THIS:

God will provide everything I need.

NOT THAT:

I'm not going to have enough to provide for myself and my family.

And my God shall supply all your need according to His riches in glory by Christ Jesus.
PHILIPPIANS 4:19

He Who did not spare His own Son, but delivered Him up for us all, how shall He not with Him also freely give us all things?
ROMANS 8:32

The young lions lack and suffer hunger; but those who seek the LORD shall not lack any good thing.
PSALM 34:10

The LORD will command the blessing on you in your storehouses and in all to which you set your hand, and He will bless you in the land which the LORD your God is giving you.
DEUTERONOMY 28:8

Give, and it will be given to you: good measure, pressed down, shaken together, and running over will be put into your bosom. For with the same measure that you use, it will be measured back to you.
LUKE 6:38

But seek first the kingdom of God and His righteousness, and all these things shall be added to you.
MATTHEW 6:33

And God is able to make all grace abound toward you, that you, always having all sufficiency in all things, may have an abundance for every good work.
2 CORINTHIANS 9:8

. . . as His divine power has given to us all things that pertain to life and godliness, through the knowledge of Him Who called us by glory and virtue.
2 PETER 1:3

Let the LORD be magnified, Who has pleasure in the prosperity of His servant.
PSALM 35:27

THINK THIS:

I am a new creation in Christ Jesus,
transformed, and renewed.

NOT THAT:

I'm going to fall back into old
habits and bad patterns.

And do not be conformed to this world, but be
transformed by the renewing of your mind, that
you may prove what is that good and acceptable
and perfect will of God.
ROMANS 12:2

Therefore, if anyone is in Christ, he is a new creation; old things have passed away; behold, all
things have become new.
2 CORINTHIANS 5:17

. . . teaching us that, denying ungodliness and
worldly lusts, we should live soberly, righteously,
and godly in the present age, looking for the
blessed hope and glorious appearing of our great
God and Savior Jesus Christ . . .
TITUS 2:12–13

Do not lie to one another, since you have put off the
old man with his deeds, and have put on the new
man who is renewed in knowledge according to the
image of Him Who created him . . .
COLOSSIANS 3:9–10

But you are a chosen generation, a royal priesthood, a holy nation, His own special people, that you may proclaim the praises of Him Who called you out of darkness into His marvelous light . . .
1 PETER 2:9

Then He said to them all, "If anyone desires to come after Me, let him deny himself, and take up his cross daily, and follow Me. For whoever desires to save his life will lose it, but whoever loses his life for My sake will save it. For what profit is it to a man if he gains the whole world, and is himself destroyed or lost?"
LUKE 9:23–25

I have been crucified with Christ; it is no longer I who live, but Christ lives in me; and the life which I now live in the flesh I live by faith in the Son of God, Who loved me and gave Himself for me.
GALATIANS 2:20

 **THINK THIS:**

Nothing is impossible for God.

 NOT THAT:

**This problem is too big;
I don't see a way out.**

For God is the King of all the earth; sing praises with understanding. God reigns over the nations;

God sits on His holy throne. The princes of the people have gathered together, the people of the God of Abraham. For the shields of the earth belong to God; He is greatly exalted.

PSALM 47:7–9

The LORD is near to those who have a broken heart, and saves such as have a contrite spirit. Many are the afflictions of the righteous, but the LORD delivers him out of them all.

PSALM 34:18–19

Great is the LORD, and greatly to be praised in the city of our God, in His holy mountain.

PSALM 48:1

He has put a new song in my mouth — Praise to our God; many will see it and fear, and will trust in the LORD.

PSALM 40:3

The LORD is your keeper; the LORD is your shade at your right hand. The sun shall not strike you by day, nor the moon by night. The LORD shall preserve you from all evil; He shall preserve your soul. The LORD shall preserve your going out and your coming in from this time forth, and even forevermore.

PSALM 121:5–8

All that the Father gives Me will come to Me, and the one who comes to Me I will by no means cast out.

JOHN 6:37

The earth is the LORD's, and all its fullness, the world and those who dwell therein. For He has founded it upon the seas, and established it upon the waters. Who may ascend into the hill of the LORD? Or who may stand in His holy place? He who has clean hands and a pure heart, who has not lifted up his soul to an idol, nor sworn deceitfully. He shall receive blessing from the LORD, and righteousness from the God of his salvation.
PSALM 24:1–5

THINK THIS:

God is guiding my steps, opening doors of opportunity, lining up the right connections.

NOT THAT:

I just don't know what to do.

I will instruct you and teach you in the way you should go; I will guide you with My eye.
PSALM 32:8

Your ears shall hear a word behind you, saying, "This is the way, walk in it," whenever you turn to the right hand or whenever you turn to the left.
ISAIAH 30:21

If any of you lacks wisdom, let him ask of God, Who gives to all liberally and without reproach, and it will be given to him. But let him ask in faith, with no

doubting, for he who doubts is like a wave of the sea driven and tossed by the wind. For let not that man suppose that he will receive anything from the Lord; he is a double-minded man, unstable in all his ways.
JAMES 1:5–8

Cast your burden on the LORD, and He shall sustain you; He shall never permit the righteous to be moved.
PSALM 55:22

For God has not give us a spirit of fear, but of power and of love and of a sound mind.
2 TIMOTHY 1:7

Trust in the LORD with all your heart, and lean not on your own understanding; in all your ways acknowledge Him, and He shall direct your paths.
PROVERBS 3:5–6

Be anxious for nothing, but in everything by prayer and supplication, with thanksgiving, let your requests be made known to God; and the peace of God, which surpasses all understanding, will guard your hearts and minds through Christ Jesus.
PHILIPPIANS 4:6–7

Great peace have those who love Your law, and nothing causes them to stumble.
PSALM 119:165

And let the peace of God rule in your hearts . . .
COLOSSIANS 3:15

Beloved, do not think it strange concerning the fiery trail which is to try you, as though some strange thing happened to you; but rejoice to the extent that you partake of Christ's sufferings, that when His glory is revealed, you may also be glad with exceeding joy.
1 PETER 4:12–13

 **THINK THIS:**

> **Because God is with me,
> I have nothing to fear.**

 NOT THAT:

> **I can't shake these feelings
> of worry and fear.**

There is no fear in love; but perfect love casts our fear, because fear involves torment. But he who fears has not been made perfect in love.
1 JOHN 4:18

Yea, though I walk through the valley of the shadow of death, I will fear no evil; for You are with me; your rod and Your staff, they comfort me. You prepare a table before me in the presence of my enemies; You anoint my head with oil; my cup runs over.
PSALM 23:4–5

For I am persuaded that neither death nor life, nor angels nor principalities nor powers, nor things present nor things to come, nor height nor depth, nor any other created thing, shall be able to separate us from the love of God which is in Christ Jesus our LORD.
ROMANS 8:35–39

No evil shall befall you, nor shall any plague come near your dwelling; for He shall give His angels charge over you, to keep you in all your ways.
PSALM 91:10–11

Peace I leave with you, My peace I give to you; not as the world gives do I give to you. Let not your heart be troubled, neither let it be afraid.
JOHN 14:27

I sought the LORD, and He heard me, and delivered me from all my fears.
PSALM 34:4

In God I have put my trust; I will not be afraid. What can man do to me?
PSALM 56:11

Fear not, for I am with you . . .
ISAIAH 41:10

The LORD is my light and my salvation; whom shall I fear? The LORD is the strength of my life; of whom shall I be afraid?
PSALM 27:1

For you did not receive the spirit of bondage again to fear, but you received the Spirit of adoption by Whom we cry out, "Abba, Father."
ROMANS 8:15

He shall cover you with His feathers, and under His wings you shall take refuge; His truth shall be your shield and buckler. You shall not be afraid of the terror by night, nor of the arrow that flies by day, nor of the pestilence that walks in darkness, nor of the destruction that lays waste at noonday. A thousand may fall at your side, and ten thousand at your right hand; but it shall not come near you.
PSALM 91:4–7

 **THINK THIS:**

> God loves me unconditionally, and He will surround me with the right people.

 NOT THAT:

> No one cares what happens to me.

God sets the solitary in families; He brings out those who are bound into prosperity; but the rebellious dwell in a dry land.
PSALM 68:6

"For the mountains shall depart the hills be removed, but My kindness shall not depart from you, nor shall

My covenant of peace be removed," says the LORD, Who has mercy on you.
ISAIAH 54:10

God is our refuge and strength, a very present help in trouble.
PSALM 46:1

When my father and my mother forsake me, then the LORD will take care of me.
PSALM 27:10

I will not leave you orphans; I will come to you.
JOHN 14:18

Lo, I am with you always, even to the end of the age. Amen.
MATTHEW 28:20

Let your conduct be without covetousness; be content with such things as you have. For He Himself has said, "I will never leave you nor forsake you."
HEBREWS 13:5

For the LORD will not forsake His people, for His great name's sake, because it has pleased the LORD to make you His people.
1 SAMUEL 12:22

Where can I go from Your Spirit? Or where can I flee from Your presence? If I ascend into heaven, You are there; if I make my bed in hell, behold, You

are there. If I take the wings of the morning, and dwell in the uttermost parts of the sea, even there Your hand shall lead me, and Your right hand shall hold me. If I say, "Surely the darkness shall fall on me," even the night shall be light about me; indeed, the darkness shall not hide from You, but the night shines as the day; the darkness and the light are both alike to You.
PSALM 139:7–12

God is my strength. He has equipped me with everything I need.

I don't have the strength to keep going.

Cast your burden on the LORD, and He shall sustain you; He shall never permit the righteous to be moved.
PSALM 55:22

Then surely you could lift up your face without spot; yes, you could be steadfast, and not fear . . .
JOB 11:15

Now to Him Who is able to keep you from stumbling, and to present you faultless before the presence of His glory with exceeding joy . . .
JUDE 1:24

I have set the LORD always before me; because He is at my right hand I shall not be moved.
PSALM 16:8

Therefore, my beloved brethren, be steadfast, immovable, always abounding in the work of the Lord, knowing that your labor is not in vain in the Lord.
1 CORINTHIANS 15:58

Seeing then that we have a great High Priest Who has passed through the heavens, Jesus the Son of God, let us hold fast our confession.
HEBREWS 4:14

My flesh and my heart fail; but God is the strength of my heart and my portion forever.
PSALM 73:26

 **THINK THIS:**
God has freedom and
breakthrough in store for me.

 NOT THAT:
There's no way I can overcome
this addiction.

My grace is sufficient for you, for My strength is made perfect in weakness.
2 CORINTHIANS 12:9

Let the words of my mouth and the meditation of my heart be acceptable in Your sight, O LORD, my strength and my Redeemer.
PSALM 19:14

I have been crucified with Christ; it is no longer I who live, but Christ lives in me; and the life which I now live in the flesh I live by faith in the Son of God, Who loved me and gave Himself for me.
GALATIANS 2:20

Confess your trespasses to one another, and pray for one another, that you may be healed.
JAMES 5:16

Humble yourselves in the sight of the Lord, and He will lift you up.
JAMES 4:10

For I know that in me (that is, in my flesh) nothing good dwells; for to will is present with me, but how to perform what is good I do not find. I find then a law, that evil is present with me, the one who wills to do good. For I delight in the law of God according to the inward man.
ROMANS 7:18, 21–22

Search me, O God, and know my heart; try me, and know my anxieties; and see if there is any wicked way in me, and lead me in the way everlasting.
PSALM 139:23–24

There is therefore now no condemnation to those who are in Christ Jesus, who do not walk according to the flesh, but according to the Spirit. For the law of the Spirit of life in Christ Jesus has made me free from the law of sin and death. For what the law could not do in that it was weak through the flesh, God did by sending His own Son in the likeness of sinful flesh, on account of sin: He condemned sin in the flesh, that the righteous requirement of the law might be fulfilled in us who do not walk according to the flesh but according to the Spirit.

ROMANS 8:1–4

The Lord is faithful, Who will establish you and guard you from the evil one.

2 THESSALONIANS 3:3

 *THINK THIS:*

I know God is making a way for me even when there seems to be no way.

 NOT THAT:

I don't think I can take anymore; I'm ready to give up.

But those who wait on the LORD shall renew their strength; they shall mount up with wings like eagles, they shall run and not be weary, they shall walk and not faint.

ISAIAH 40:31

Wait on the LORD; be of good courage, and He shall strengthen your heart; wait, I say, on the LORD!
PSALM 27:14

My brethren, count it all joy when you fall into various trials, knowing that the testing of your faith produces patience. But let patience have its perfect work, that you may be perfect and complete, lacking nothing.
JAMES 1:2–4

And He said, "My Presence will go with you, and I will give you rest."
EXODUS 33:14

I cried to the LORD with my voice, and He heard me from His holy hill. I lay down and slept; I awoke, for the LORD sustained me.
PSALM 3:4–5

My soul waits for the Lord more than those who watch for the morning — yes, more than those who watch for the morning.
PSALM 130:6

Therefore be patient, brethren, until the coming of the Lord. See how the farmer waits for the precious fruit of the earth, waiting patiently for it until it receives the early and latter rain. You also be patient. Establish your hearts, for the coming of the Lord is at hand.
JAMES 5:7–8

And so, after he had patiently endured, he obtained the promise.
HEBREWS 6:15

 **THINK THIS:**

I choose hope over worry, faith over fear.

 NOT THAT:

I never get a break from worrying about my troubles.

Blessed is the man who trusts in the LORD, and whose hope is the LORD. For he shall be like a tree planted by the waters, which spreads out its roots by the river, and will not fear when heat comes; but its leaf will be green, and will not be anxious in the year of drought, nor will cease from yielding fruit.
JEREMIAH 17:7–8

Look at the birds of the air, for they neither sow nor reap nor gather into barns; yet your heavenly Father feeds them. Are you not of more value than they?
MATTHEW 6:26

Do not labor for the food which perishes, but for the food which endures to everlasting life, which the Son of Man will give you, because God the Father has set His seal on Him.
JOHN 6:27

Therefore I say to you, do not worry about your life, what you will eat or what you will drink; nor about your body, what you will put on. Is not life more than food and the body more than clothing?
MATTHEW 6:25

Let your conduct be without covetousness; be content with such things as you have. For He Himself has said, "I will never leave you nor forsake you."
HEBREWS 13:5

. . . casting all your care upon Him, for He cares for you.
1 PETER 5:7

But I want you to be without care.
1 CORINTHIANS 7:32

Anxiety in the heart of a man causes depression, but a good word makes it glad.
PROVERBS 12:25

2

MY RELATIONSHIPS

THINK THIS:

> God can heal my heart and bring
> me out better than before.

 NOT THAT:

> I don't see how I can ever get over the
> pain of this broken relationship.

The LORD is near to those who have a broken heart,
and saves such as have a contrite spirit.
PSALM 34:18

Blessed be the God and Father of our Lord Jesus
Christ, the Father of mercies and God of all comfort, Who comforts us in all our tribulation, that
we may be able to comfort those who are in any
trouble, with the comfort with which we ourselves
are comforted by God.
2 CORINTHIANS 1:3–4

Sing, O heavens! Be joyful, O earth! And break out in
singing, O mountains! For the LORD has comforted
His people, and will have mercy on His afflicted.
ISAIAH 49:13

The Spirit of the Lord GOD is upon Me, because
the LORD has anointed Me to preach good tidings
to the poor; He has sent Me to heal the brokenhearted, to proclaim liberty to the captives, and the
opening of the prison to those who are bound; to
proclaim the acceptable year of the LORD, and the
day of vengeance of our God; to comfort all who

mourn, to console those who mourn in Zion, to give them beauty for ashes, the oil of joy for mourning, the garment of praise for the spirit of heaviness; that they may be called trees of righteousness, the planting of the LORD, that He may be glorified.
ISAIAH 61:1–3

When you pass through the waters, I will be with you; and through the rivers, they shall not overflow you. When you walk through the fire, you shall not be burned, nor shall the flame scorch you.
ISAIAH 43:2

Yea, though I walk through the valley of the shadow of death, I will fear no evil; for You are with me; Your rod and Your staff, they comfort me.
PSALM 23:4

And God will wipe away every tear from their eyes; there shall be no more death, nor sorrow, nor crying. There shall be no more pain, for the former things have passed away.
REVELATION 21:4

 **THINK THIS:**

I am going to bring peace, encouragement, and a good attitude into my encounters with others today.

 NOT THAT:

These constant struggles with people who are supposed to be my friends are driving me crazy.

For God is not the author of confusion but of peace, as in all the churches of the saints.
1 CORINTHIANS 14:33

Who is the man who desires life, and loves many days, that he may see good? Keep your tongue from evil, and your lips from speaking deceit. Depart from evil and do good; seek peace and pursue it.
PSALM 34:12–14

Be at peace among yourselves.
1 THESSALONIANS 5:13

He makes peace in your borders, and fills you with the finest wheat.
PSALM 147:14

I form the light and create darkness, I make peace and create calamity; I, the LORD, do all these things.
ISAIAH 45:7

When a man's ways please the LORD, He makes even his enemies to be at peace with him.
PROVERBS 16:7

Flee also youthful lusts; but pursue righteousness, faith, love, peace with those who call on the Lord out of a pure heart.
2 TIMOTHY 2:22

For [he] who would love life and see good days, let him refrain his tongue from evil, and his lips from speaking deceit. Let him turn away from evil and do good; let him seek peace and pursue it.
1 PETER 3:10–11

Behold, how good and how pleasant it is for brethren to dwell together in unity!
PSALM 133:1

My soul has dwelt too long with one who hates peace. I am for peace; but when I speak, they are for war.
PSALM 120:6–7

 **THINK THIS:**
I'm going to do what is right, regardless of what others do or how they treat me.

 NOT THAT:
Nobody treats me right; why should I treat others any better?

Let all bitterness, wrath, anger, clamor, and evil speaking be put away from you, with all malice. And be kind to one another, tenderhearted, forgiving one another, ever as God in Christ forgave you.
EPHESIANS 4:31–32

Therefore, whatever you want men to do to you, do also to them, for this is the Law and the Prophets.
MATTHEW 7:12

Love suffers long and is kind; loves does not envy; love does not parade itself, is not puffed up; does not behave rudely, does not see its own, is not provoked, thins no evil; does not rejoice in iniquity, but rejoices in the truth; bears all things, believes all things, hopes all things, endures all things.
1 CORINTHIANS 13:4–7

He has shown you, O man, what is good; and what does the LORD require of you but to do justly, to love mercy, and to walk humbly with your God?
MICAH 6:8

He who walks righteously and speaks uprightly, he who despises the gain of oppressions, who gestures with his hands, refusing bribes, who stops his ears from hearing of bloodshed, and shuts his eyes from seeing evil: he will dwell on high; his place of defense will be the fortress of rocks; bread will be given him, his water will be sure.
ISAIAH 33:15–16

So he answered and said, "You shall love the LORD your God with all your heart, with all your soul, with all your strength, and with all your mind, and your neighbor as yourself."
LUKE 10:27

But love your enemies, do good, and lend, hoping for nothing in return; and your reward will be great, and you will be sons of the Most High. For He is kind to the unthankful and evil.
LUKE 6:35

And let us not grow weary while doing good, for in due season we shall reap if we do not lose heart.
GALATIANS 6:9

 **THINK THIS:**

I'm going to surround myself with people who will encourage me to pursue my destiny.

42

 NOT THAT:

I'm pretty self-sufficient; I don't need anybody.

Therefore comfort each other and edify one another, just as you also are doing.
1 THESSALONIANS 5:11

I do not pray for these alone, but also for those who will believe in Me through their word; that they all may be one, as You, Father, are in Me, and I in You; that they also may be one in Us, that the world may believe that You sent Me.
JOHN 17:20–21

For where two or three are gathered together in My name, I am there in the midst of them.
MATTHEW 18:20

Then those who feared the LORD spoke to one another, and the LORD listened and heard them, so a book of remembrance was written before Him for those who fear the LORD and who meditate on His name.
MALACHI 3:16

We took sweet counsel together, and walked to the house of God in the throng.
PSALM 55:14

These all continued with one accord in prayer and supplication, with the women and Mary the mother of Jesus, and with His brothers.
ACTS 1:14

. . . not forsaking the assembling of ourselves together, as is the manner of some, but exhorting one another, and so much the more as you see the Day approaching.
HEBREWS 10:25

For we, though many, are one bread and one body; for we all partake of that one bread.
1 CORINTHIANS 10:17

. . . you also helping together in prayer for us, that thanks may be given by many persons on our behalf for the gift granted to us through many.
2 CORINTHIANS 1:11

As for the saints who are on the earth, they are the excellent ones, in whom is all my delight.
PSALM 16:3

I, therefore, the prisoner of the Lord, beseech you to walk worthy of the calling with which you were called, with all lowliness and gentleness, with longsuffering, bearing with one another in love, endeavoring to keep the unity of the Spirit in the bond of peace.
EPHESIANS 4:1–3

I choose to see people the way God sees them and love them unconditionally.

I just can't get along with these people.

He who loves his brother abides in the light, and there is no cause for stumbling in him. But he

who hates his brother is in darkness and walks in darkness, and does not know where he is going, because the darkness has blinded his eyes.
1 JOHN 2:9–11

But you are a chosen generation, a royal priesthood, a holy nation, His own special people, that you may proclaim the praises of Him Who called you out of darkness into His marvelous light . . .
1 PETER 2:9

God is faithful, by Whom you were called into the fellowship of His Son, Jesus Christ our Lord. Now I plead with you, brethren, by the name of our Lord Jesus Christ, that you all speak the same thing, and that there be no divisions among you, but that you be perfectly joined together in the same mind and in the same judgment.
1 CORINTHIANS 1:9–10

But now indeed there are many members, yet one body.
1 CORINTHIANS 12:20

If we say that we have fellowship with Him, and walk in darkness, we lie and do not practice the truth. But if we walk in the light as He is in the light, we have fellowship with one another, and the blood of Jesus Christ His Son cleanses us from all sin.
1 JOHN 1:6–7

But God, Who is rich in mercy, because of His great love with which He loved us, even when we were dead in trespasses, made us alive together with Christ (by grace you have been saved), and raised us up together, and made us sit together in the heavenly places in Christ Jesus . . .
EPHESIANS 2:4–6

 *THINK THIS:*

God is my vindication, my protector, and my redeemer.

 NOT THAT:

I want to get even for what was done to me — I deserve revenge.

You shall not take vengeance, nor bear any grudge against the children of your people, but you shall love your neighbor as yourself: I am the LORD.
LEVITICUS 19:18

Repay no one evil for evil. Have regard for good things in the sight of all men. If it is possible, as much as depends on you, live peaceably with all men. Beloved, do not avenge yourselves, but rather give place to wrath; for it is written, "Vengeance is Mine, I will repay," says the Lord.
ROMANS 12:17–19

Do not rejoice when your enemy falls, and do not let your heart be glad when he stumbles . . .
PROVERBS 24:17

. . . not returning evil for evil or reviling for reviling, but on the contrary blessing, knowing that you were called to this, that you may inherit a blessing.
1 PETER 3:9

Bless those who persecute you; bless and do not curse.
ROMANS 12:14

But I tell you not to resist an evil person. But whoever slaps you on your right cheek, turn the other to him also. If anyone wants to sue you and take away your tunic, let him have your cloak also. And whoever compels you to go one mile, go with him two.
MATTHEW 5:39–41

And when His disciples James and John saw this, they said, "Lord, do You want us to command fire to come down from heaven and consume them, just as Elijah did?" But He turned and rebuked them, and said, "You do not know what manner of spirit you are of."
LUKE 9:54–55

But love your enemies, do good, and lend, hoping for nothing in return; and your reward will be great,

and you will be sons of the Most High. For He is kind to the unthankful and evil.
LUKE 6:35

Thus says the LORD: "For three transgressions of Edom, and for four, I will not turn away its punishment, because he pursued his brother with the sword, and cast off all pity; his anger tore perpetually, and he kept his wrath forever."
AMOS 1:11

Do not say, "I will recompense evil;" wait for the LORD, and He will save you.
PROVERBS 20:22

 **THINK THIS:**

> I am going to celebrate the good things
> that happen to others, and I know God
> has good things in store for me too.

 NOT THAT:

> I can't believe they have so
> much while I have so little.

A sound heart is life to the body, but envy is rottenness to the bones.
PROVERBS 14:30

For wrath kills a foolish man, and envy slays a simple one.
JOB 5:2

Let us walk properly, as in the day, not in revelry and drunkenness, not in lewdness and lust, not in strife and envy.
ROMANS 13:13

He is proud, knowing nothing, but is obsessed with disputes and arguments over words, from which come envy, strife, reviling, evil suspicions . . .
1 TIMOTHY 6:4

Wrath is cruel and anger a torrent, but who is able to stand before jealousy?
PROVERBS 27:4

Therefore, laying aside all malice, all deceit, hypocrisy, envy, and all evil speaking, as newborn babes, desire the pure milk of the word, that you may grow thereby . . .
1 PETER 2:1–2

Let love be without hypocrisy. Abhor what is evil. Cling to what is good. Be kindly affectionate to one another with brotherly love, in honor giving preference to one another; not lagging in diligence, fervent in spirit, serving the Lord; rejoicing in hope, patient in tribulation, continuing steadfastly in prayer; distributing to the needs of the saints, given to hospitality. Bless those who persecute you; bless and do not curse. Rejoice with those who rejoice, and weep with those who weep.
ROMANS 12:9–15

THINK THIS:

God is bringing the right people into my life.

NOT THAT:

I will never find a true friend.

A friend loves at all times, and a brother is born for adversity.
PROVERBS 17:17

For as the body is one and has many members, but all the members of that one body, being many, are one body, so also is Christ.
1 CORINTHIANS 12:12

Let brotherly love continue. Do not forget to entertain strangers, for by so doing some have unwittingly entertained angels.
HEBREWS 13:1&2

Everyone helped his neighbor, and said to his brother, "Be of good courage!"
ISAIAH 41:6

Two are better than one, because they have a good reward for their labor.
ECCLESIASTES 4:9

For whoever does the will of My Father in heaven is My brother and sister and mother.
MATTHEW 12:50

Let all that you do be done with love.
1 CORINTHIANS 16:14

For you, brethren, have been called to liberty; only do not use liberty as an opportunity for the flesh, but through love serve one another.
GALATIANS 5:13

This is My commandment, that you love one another as I have loved you. Greater love has no one than this, than to lay down one's life for his friends.
JOHN 15:12–13

And if one member suffers, all the members suffer with it; or if one member is honored, all the members rejoice with it.
1 CORINTHIANS 12:26

 **THINK THIS:**
Success, favor, promotion, and increase are coming my way because God has a good plan for my life.

 NOT THAT:
I have to compete with others in order to be successful.

A new commandment I give to you, that you love one another; as I have loved you, that you also

love one another. By this all will know that you are My disciples, if you have love for one another.
JOHN 13:34-35

And whatever you do, do it heartily, as to the Lord and not to men, knowing that from the Lord you will receive the reward of the inheritance; for you serve the Lord Christ. But he who does wrong will be repaid for what he has done, and there is no partiality.
COLOSSIANS 3:23-25

And whoever desires to be first among you, let him be your slave — just as the Son of Man did not come to be served, but to serve, and to give His life a ransom for many.
MATTHEW 20:27-28

And now, little children, abide in Him, that when He appears, we may have confidence and not be ashamed before Him at His coming.
1 JOHN 2:28

For you, brethren, have been called to liberty; only do not use liberty as an opportunity for the flesh, but through love serve one another.
GALATIANS 5:13

He who is faithful in what is least is faithful also in much; and he who is unjust in what is least is unjust also in much. Therefore if you have not been faithful in the unrighteous mammon, who will commit

to your trust the true riches? And if you have not been faithful in what is another man's, who will give you what is your own? No servant can serve two masters; for either he will hate the one and love the other, or else he will be loyal to the one and despise the other. You cannot serve God and mammon.
LUKE 16:10–13

A sound heart is life to the body, As each one has received a gift, minister it to one another, as good stewards of the manifold grace of God. If anyone speaks, let him speak as the oracles of God. If anyone ministers, let him do it as with the ability which God supplies, that in all things God may be glorified through Jesus Christ, to Whom belong the glory and the dominion forever and ever. Amen.
1 PETER 4:10–11

THINK THIS:
I'm going to see the value in others and put their needs ahead of my own, knowing God will take care of me.

NOT THAT:
People should do things the way I want them to.

Love suffers long and is kind; love does not envy; love does not parade itself, is not puffed up; does

not behave rudely, does not seek its own, is not provoked, thinks no evil . . .
1 CORINTHIANS 13:4–5

You shall love your neighbor as yourself.
MATTHEW 22:39

If you really fulfill the royal law according to the Scripture, "You shall love your neighbor as yourself," you do well . . .
JAMES 2:8

For as we have many members in one body, but all the members do not have the same function, so we, being many, are one body in Christ, and individually members of one another.
ROMANS 12:4–5

. . . just as I also please all men in all things, not seeking my own profit, but the profit of many, that they may be saved.
1 CORINTHIANS 10:33

Therefore if there is any consolation in Christ, if any comfort of love, if any fellowship of the Spirit, if any affection and mercy, fulfill my joy by being like-minded, having the same love, being of one accord, of one mind. Let nothing be done through selfish ambition or conceit, but in lowliness of mind let each esteem others better than himself. Let each of you look out not only for his own interests, but also for the interests of others.
PHILIPPIANS 2:1–4

3

MY FEELINGS

THINK THIS:

I may feel angry about something, but I'm not going to let anger rule my life.

NOT THAT:

I'm so angry over how I was treated.

He who is slow to anger is better than the mighty, and he who rules his spirit than he who takes a city.
PROVERBS 16:32

Let all bitterness, wrath, anger, clamor, and evil speaking be put away from you, with all malice. And be kind to one another, tenderhearted, forgiving one another, even as God in Christ forgave you.
EPHESIANS 4:31-32

"Be angry, and do not sin": do not let the sun go down on your wrath . . .
EPHESIANS 4:26

My beloved brethren, let every man be swift to hear, slow to speak, slow to wrath; for the wrath of man does not produce the righteousness of God.
JAMES 1:19-20

A wise man fears and departs from evil, but a fool rages and is self-confident. A quick-tempered man acts foolishly, and a man of wicked intentions is hated.
PROVERBS 14:16-17

Where envy and self-seeking exist, confusion and every evil thing are there. But the wisdom that is from above is first pure, then peaceable, gentle, willing to yield, full of mercy and good fruits, without partiality and without hypocrisy. Now the fruit of righteousness is sown in peace by those who make peace.

JAMES 3:16–18

A soft answer turns away wrath, but a harsh word stirs up anger.

PROVERBS 15:1

Cease from anger, and forsake wrath; do not fret — it only causes harm.

PSALM 37:8

 **THINK THIS:**

I am a child of Almighty God — loved, forgiven, redeemed, and righteous in His sight.

 NOT THAT:

I'll never get over this feeling of guilt for what I've done.

If we confess our sins, He is faithful and just to forgive us our sins and to cleanse us from all unrighteousness.

1 JOHN 1:9

You will cast all our sins into the depths of the sea.
MICAH 7:19

The LORD your God is gracious and merciful, and will not turn His face from you if you return to Him.
2 CHRONICLES 30:9

If anyone is in Christ, he is a new creation; old things have passed away; behold, all things have become new.
2 CORINTHIANS 5:17

He has not dealt with us according to our sins, nor punished us according to our iniquities.
PSALM 103:10

Let us draw near with a true heart in full assurance of faith, having our hearts sprinkled from an evil conscience and our bodies washed with pure water.
HEBREWS 10:22

Most assuredly, I say to you, he who hears My word and believes in Him Who sent Me has everlasting life, and shall not come into judgment, but has passed from death into life.
JOHN 5:24

Let the wicked forsake his way, and the unrighteous man his thoughts; let him return to the LORD, and He will have mercy on him; and to our God, for He will abundantly pardon.
ISAIAH 55:7

If anyone sins, we have an Advocate with the Father, Jesus Christ the righteous. And He Himself is the propitiation for our sins, and not for ours only but also for the whole world.

1 JOHN 2:1–2

God did not send His Son into the world to condemn the world, but that the world through Him might be saved. He who believes in Him is not condemned; but he who does not believe is condemned already, because he has not believed in the name of the only begotten Son of God.

JOHN 3:17–18

 **THINK THIS:**

I am going to stay humble, keep doing my best, and remember that God is the source of any success I have.

 NOT THAT:

I've got it all together right now; others should look up to me.

Talk no more so very proudly; let no arrogance come from your mouth, for the LORD is the God of knowledge; and by Him actions are weighed.

1 SAMUEL 2:3

These six things the LORD hates, yes, seven are an abomination to Him: a proud look, a lying tongue, hands that shed innocent blood . . .
PROVERBS 6:16–17

Knowledge puffs up, but love edifies. And if anyone thinks that he knows anything, he knows nothing yet as he ought to know.
1 CORINTHIANS 8:1–2

The fear of the LORD is to hate evil; pride and arrogance and the evil way and the perverse mouth I hate.
PROVERBS 8:13

For I say, through the grace given to me, to everyone who is among you, not to think of himself more highly than he ought to think, but to think soberly, as God has dealt to each one a measure of faith.
ROMANS 12:3

For from within, out of the heart of men, proceed evil thoughts, adulteries, fornications, murders, thefts, covetousness, wickedness, deceit, lewdness, an evil eye, blasphemy, pride, foolishness. All these evil things come from within and defile a man.
MARK 7:21–23

Hear and give ear: Do not be proud, for the LORD has spoken.
JEREMIAH 13:15

But when his heart was lifted up, and his spirit was hardened in pride, he was deposed from his kingly throne, and they took his glory from him.
DANIEL 5:20

The wicked in his proud countenance does not seek God; God is in none of his thoughts.
PSALM 10:4

 *THINK THIS:*

I have nothing to fear because God is
with me. He has a good plan for my life.

 NOT THAT:

This dark cloud over my life
will never go away.

Fear not, for I am with you; be not dismayed, for I am your God. I will strengthen you, yes, I will help you, I will uphold you with My righteous right hand.
ISAIAH 41:10

Blessed be the God and Father of our Lord Jesus Christ, the Father of mercies and God of all comfort, Who comforts us in all our tribulation, that we may be able to comfort those who are in any trouble, with the comfort with which we ourselves are comforted by God.
2 CORINTHIANS 1:3–4

The ransomed of the LORD shall return, and come to Zion with singing, with everlasting joy on their heads. They shall obtain joy and gladness; sorrow and sighing shall flee away.
ISAIAH 51:11

This day is holy to our Lord. Do not sorrow, for the joy of the LORD is your strength.
NEHEMIAH 8:10

He spoke a parable to them, that men always ought to pray and not lose heart . . .
LUKE 18:1

Those who wait on the LORD shall renew their strength; they shall mount up with wings like eagles, they shall run and not be weary, they shall walk and not faint.
ISAIAH 40:31

Finally, brethren, whatever things are true, whatever things are noble, whatever things are just, whatever things are pure, whatever things are lovely, whatever things are of good report, if there is any virtue and if there is anything praiseworthy — meditate on these things.
PHILIPPIANS 4:8

To console those who mourn in Zion, to give them beauty for ashes, the oil of joy for mourning, the garment of praise for the spirit of heaviness; that

they may be called trees of righteousness, the planting of the LORD, that He may be glorified.
ISAIAH 61:3

His anger is but for a moment, His favor is for life; weeping may endure for a night, but joy comes in the morning.
PSALM 30:5

 **THINK THIS:**

I choose to live my life happy and bloom where I'm planted. The joy of the Lord is my strength.

 NOT THAT:

I don't feel like I'm ever going to be happy.

You have put gladness in my heart, more than in the season that their grain and wine increased.
PSALM 4:7

For God gives wisdom and knowledge and joy to a man who is good in His sight; but to the sinner He gives the work of gathering and collecting, that he may give to him who is good before God. This also is vanity and grasping for the wind.
ECCLESIASTES 2:26

Finally, my brethren, rejoice in the Lord. For me to write the same things to you is not tedious, but for you it is safe.
PHILIPPIANS 3:1

And they worshiped Him, and returned to Jerusalem with great joy . . .
LUKE 24:52

The humble also shall increase their joy in the LORD, and the poor among men shall rejoice in the Holy One of Israel.
ISAIAH 29:19

And not only that, but we also rejoice in God through our Lord Jesus Christ, through Whom we have now received the reconciliation.
ROMANS 5:11

Your words were found, and I ate them, and Your word was to me the joy and rejoicing of my heart; for I am called by Your name, O LORD God of hosts.
JEREMIAH 15:16

Light is sown for the righteous, and gladness for the upright in heart.
PSALM 97:11

Now when he had brought them into his house, he set food before them; and he rejoiced, having believed in God with all his household.
ACTS 16:34

And all the people went their way to eat and drink, to send portions and rejoice greatly, because they understood the words that were declared to them.
NEHEMIAH 8:12

Yet I will rejoice in the LORD, I will joy in the God of my salvation.
HABAKKUK 3:18

 *THINK THIS:*

God has done good things in my life, and He has even greater things in store.

 NOT THAT:

What do I have to be joyful about?

You have put gladness in my heart, blessed is every one who fears the LORD, who walks in His ways. When you eat the labor of your hands, you shall be happy, and it shall be well with you.
PSALM 128:1–2

Whom have I in heaven but You? And there is none upon earth that I desire besides You. My flesh and my heart fail; but God is the strength of my heart and my portion forever.
PSALM 73:25–26

Her ways are ways of pleasantness, and all her paths are peace. She is a tree of life to those who take hold of her, and happy are all who retain her.
PROVERBS 3:17–18

Those who sow in tears shall reap in joy.
PSALM 126:5

He who heeds the word wisely will find good, and whoever trusts in the LORD, happy is he.
PROVERBS 16:20

Be anxious for nothing, but in everything by prayer and supplication, with thanksgiving, let your requests be made known to God; and the peace of God, which surpasses all understanding, will guard your hearts and minds through Christ Jesus.
PHILIPPIANS 4:6–7

But now I come to You, and these things I speak in the world, that they may have My joy fulfilled in themselves.
JOHN 17:13

If you know these things, blessed are you if you do them.
JOHN 13:17

I delight to do Your will, O my God, and Your law is within my heart.
PSALM 40:8

We have access by faith into this grace in which we stand, and rejoice in hope of the glory of God.
ROMANS 5:2

Happy are the people who are in such a state; happy are the people whose God is the LORD!
PSALM 144:15

 THINK THIS:
> There is an anointing of ease on my life. God is going before me to make the crooked places straight.

NOT THAT:
> I'm so tired; nothing I do ever seems to work.

Be of good courage, and He shall strengthen your heart, all you who hope in the LORD.
PSALM 31:24

We are hard-pressed on every side, yet not crushed; we are perplexed, but not in despair; persecuted, but not forsaken; struck down, but not destroyed . . .
2 CORINTHIANS 4:8–9

. . . being confident of this very thing, that He Who has begun a good work in you will complete it until the day of Jesus Christ.
PHILIPPIANS 1:6

Peace I leave with you, My peace I give to you; not as the world gives do I give to you. Let not your heart be troubled, neither let it be afraid.
JOHN 14:27

Though I walk in the midst of trouble, You will revive me; You will stretch out Your hand against the wrath of my enemies, and Your right hand will save me.
PSALM 138:7

Let us not grow weary while doing good, for in due season we shall reap if we do not lose heart.
GALATIANS 6:9

Do not cast away your confidence, which has great reward. For you have need of endurance, so that you have done the will of God, you may receive the promise.
HEBREWS 10:35–36

We were burdened beyond measure, above strength, so that we despaired even of life. Yes, we had the sentence of death in ourselves, that we should not trust in ourselves but in God Who raises the dead.
2 CORINTHIANS 1:8–9

I would have lost heart, unless I had believed that I would see the goodness of the LORD in the land of the living. Wait on the LORD; be of good courage, and He shall strengthen your heart; wait, I say, on the LORD!
PSALM 27:13–14

Come to Me, all you who labor and are heavy laden, and I will give you rest.
MATTHEW 11:28

 *THINK THIS:*

> **I'm not going to doubt the goodness of God. I choose to stay in faith and believe His promises for my life.**

 NOT THAT:

> **Doubts are consuming my mind.**

With men it is impossible, but not with God; for with God all things are possible.
MARK 10:27

Without faith it is impossible to please Him, for he who comes to God must believe that He is, and that He is a rewarder of those who diligently seek Him.
HEBREWS 11:6

If any of you lacks wisdom, let him ask of God, Who gives to all liberally and without reproach, and

it will be given to him. But let him ask in faith, with no doubting, for he who doubts is like a wave of the sea driven and tossed by the wind. For let not that man suppose that he will receive anything from the Lord; he is a double-minded man, unstable in all his ways.
JAMES 1:5–8

Abraham believed God, and it was accounted to him for righteousness.
JAMES 2:23

I am not ashamed of the gospel of Christ, for it is the power of God to salvation for everyone who believes, for the Jew first and also for the Greek. For in it the righteousness of God is revealed from faith to faith; as it is written, "The just shall live by faith."
ROMANS 1:16–17

Let us lay aside every weight, and the sin which so easily ensnares us, and let us run with endurance the race that is set before us, looking unto Jesus, the author and finisher of our faith . . .
HEBREWS 12:1–2

Jesus answered and said to them, "Have faith in God. For assuredly, I say to you, whoever says to this mountain, 'Be removed and be cast into the sea,' and does not doubt in his heart, but believes that those things he says will be done, he will have whatever he says. Therefore I say to you, whatever

things you ask when you pray, believe that you receive them, and you will have them."
MARK 11:22–24

Weeping may endure for a night, but joy comes in the morning.
PSALM 30:5

He did not waver at the promise of God through unbelief, but was strengthened in faith, giving glory to God, and being fully convinced that what He had promised He was also able to perform.
ROMANS 4:20–21

 *THINK THIS:*

God is working behind the scenes.
Favor, promotion, opportunity, and
good breaks are coming my way.

 NOT THAT:

I'm so stressed out that I can't see any hope.

Take My yoke upon you and learn from Me, for I am gentle and lowly in heart, and you will find rest for your souls. For My yoke is easy and My burden is light.
MATTHEW 11:28–30

Be still, and know that I am God . . .
PSALM 46:10

Peace I leave with you, My peace I give to you; not as the world gives do I give to you. Let not your heart be troubled, neither let it be afraid.
JOHN 14:27

Jesus Himself stood in the midst of them, and said to them, "Peace to you."
LUKE 24:36

The beloved of the LORD shall dwell in safety by Him, Who shelters him all the day long; and he shall dwell between His shoulders.
DEUTERONOMY 33:12

The weapons of our warfare are not carnal but mighty in God for pulling down strongholds, casting down arguments and every high thing that exalts itself against the knowledge of God, bringing every thought into captivity to the obedience of Christ.
2 CORINTHIANS 10:4–5

Rejoice in the Lord always. Again I will say, rejoice! Let your gentleness be known to all men. The Lord is at hand. Be anxious for nothing, but in everything by prayer and supplication, with thanksgiving, let your requests be made known to God; and the peace of God, which surpasses all understanding, will guard your hearts and minds through Christ Jesus. Finally, brethren, whatever things are true, whatever things are noble, whatever things are just, whatever things are pure, whatever things are

lovely, whatever things are of good report, if there is any virtue and if there is anything praiseworthy — meditate on these things. The things which you learned and received and heard and saw in me, these do, and the God of peace will be with you.
PHILIPPIANS 4:4–9

 **THINK THIS:**

**God is my shelter and my refuge.
I have nothing to fear.**

 NOT THAT:

My problems are going to overwhelm me.

The LORD is good, a stronghold in the day of trouble; and He knows those who trust in Him.
NAHUM 1:7

When you pass through the waters, I will be with you; and through the rivers, they shall not overflow you. When you walk through the fire, you shall not be burned, nor shall the flame scorch you.
ISAIAH 43:2

And we know that all things work together for good to those who love God, to those who are the called according to His purpose.
ROMANS 8:28

I will lift up my eyes to the hills — from whence comes my help? My help comes from the LORD, Who made heaven and earth.
PSALM 121:1–2

I will be glad and rejoice in Your mercy, for You have considered my trouble; You have known my soul in adversities.
PSALM 31:7

Therefore do not worry about tomorrow, for tomorrow will worry about its own things. Sufficient for the day is its own trouble.
MATTHEW 6:34

We are hard-pressed on every side, yet not crushed; we are perplexed, but not in despair; persecuted, but not forsaken; struck down, but not destroyed.
2 CORINTHIANS 4:8–9

From the end of the earth I will cry to You, when my heart is overwhelmed; lead me to the rock that is higher than I.
PSALM 61:2

Let not your heart be troubled; you believe in God, believe also in Me.
JOHN 14:1

Blessed be the LORD, Who has not given us as prey to their teeth. Our soul has escaped as a bird from the snare of the fowlers; the snare is broken, and we

have escaped. Our help is in the name of the LORD,
Who made heaven and earth.
PSALM 124:6–8

THINK THIS:

**God will accelerate His plan for my
life if I put my trust in Him.**

NOT THAT:

I feel paralyzed by fear and worry.

Have I not commanded you? Be strong and of good
courage; do not be afraid, nor be dismayed, for the
LORD your God is with you wherever you go.
JOSHUA 1:9

Be of good courage, and He shall strengthen your
heart, all you who hope in the LORD.
PSALM 31:24

For I am persuaded that neither death nor life, nor
angels nor principalities nor powers, nor things
present nor things to come, nor height nor depth,
nor any other created thing, shall be able to separate us from the love of God which is in Christ Jesus
our Lord.
ROMANS 8:38–39

Have you not known? Have you not heard? The
everlasting God, the LORD, the Creator of the ends

of the earth, neither faints nor is weary. His under-standing is unsearchable. He gives power to the weak, and to those who have no might He increases strength. Even the youths shall faint and be weary, and the young men shall utterly fall, but those who wait on the LORD shall renew their strength; they shall mount up with wings like eagles, they shall run and not be weary, they shall walk and not faint.
ISAIAH 40:28–31

Wait on the LORD; be of good courage, and He shall strengthen your heart; wait, I say, on the LORD!
PSALM 27:14

Beloved, do not think it strange concerning the fiery trial which is to try you, as though some strange thing happened to you; but rejoice to the extent that you partake of Christ's sufferings, that when His glory is revealed, you may also be glad with exceeding joy.
1 PETER 4:12–13

But now, thus says the LORD, Who created you, O Jacob, and He Who formed you, O Israel: "Fear not, for I have redeemed you; I have called you by your name; you are Mine. When you pass through the waters, I will be with you; and through the riv-ers, they shall not overflow you. When you walk through the fire, you shall not be burned, nor shall the flame scorch you. For I am the LORD your God, the Holy One of Israel, your Savior . . ."
ISAIAH 43:1–3

The eternal God is your refuge . . .
DEUTERONOMY 33:27

 **THINK THIS:**

Today is a new day with new
opportunities. I choose to live today
in faith, hope, strength, and joy.

 NOT THAT:

Sadness fills my mind and heart every day.

Because Your lovingkindness is better than life,
my lips shall praise You. Thus I will bless You while
I live; I will lift up my hands in Your name. My soul
shall be satisfied as with marrow and fatness, and
my mouth shall praise You with joyful lips.
PSALM 63:3–5

For the kingdom of God is not eating and drinking, but
righteousness and peace and joy in the Holy Spirit.
ROMANS 14:17

These things I have spoken to you, that My joy may
remain in you, and that your joy may be full. This is
My commandment, that you love one another as I
have loved you.
JOHN 15:11–12

A merry heart makes a cheerful countenance, but by sorrow of the heart the spirit is broken.
PROVERBS 15:13

Oh, satisfy us early with Your mercy, that we may rejoice and be glad all our days!
PSALM 90:14

Create in me a clean heart, O God, and renew a steadfast spirit within me. Do not cast me away from Your presence, and do not take Your Holy Spirit from me. Restore to me the joy of Your salvation, and uphold me by Your generous Spirit.
PSALM 51:10–12

Let us come before His presence with thanksgiving; let us shout joyfully to Him with psalms.
PSALM 95:2

This is the day the LORD has made; we will rejoice and be glad in it.
PSALM 118:24

THINK THIS:

I am the very righteousness of God in Christ Jesus. I can come boldly before His throne of grace.

NOT THAT:

I feel so much shame over the mistakes I've made.

There is therefore now no condemnation to those who are in Christ Jesus, who do not walk according to the flesh, but according to the Spirit.
ROMANS 8:1

Blessed is he whose transgression is forgiven, whose sin is covered.
PSALM 32:1

For if you return to the LORD, your brethren and your children will be treated with compassion by those who lead them captive, so that they may come back to this land; for the LORD your God is gracious and merciful, and will not turn His face from you if you return to Him.
2 CHRONICLES 30:9

No more shall every man teach his neighbor, and every man his brother, saying, 'Know the LORD,' for they all shall know Me, from the least of them to the greatest of them, says the LORD. For I will forgive their iniquity, and their sin I will remember no more.
JEREMIAH 31:34

He has not dealt with us according to our sins, nor punished us according to our iniquities. For as the heavens are high above the earth, so great is His mercy toward those who fear Him; as far as the east is from the west, so far has He removed our transgressions from us.
PSALM 103:10–12

Let the wicked forsake his way, and the unrighteous man his thoughts; let him return to the LORD, and He will have mercy on him; and to our God, for He will abundantly pardon.
ISAIAH 55:7

For God did not send His Son into the world to condemn the world, but that the world through Him might be saved. He who believes in Him is not condemned; but he who does not believe is condemned already, because he has not believed in the name of the only begotten Son of God.
JOHN 3:17–18

Let us draw near with a true heart in full assurance of faith, having our hearts sprinkled from an evil conscience and our bodies washed with pure water. Let us hold fast the confession of our hope without wavering, for He Who promised is faithful.
HEBREWS 10:22–23

I acknowledged my sin to You, and my iniquity I have not hidden. I said, "I will confess my transgres-

sions to the LORD," and You forgave the iniquity of my sin.
PSALM 32:5

I, even I, am He Who blots out your transgressions for My own sake; and I will not remember your sins.
ISAIAH 43:25

 *THINK THIS:*

> My circumstances don't determine my destiny. I'm going to keep moving forward into what God has promised for me.

 NOT THAT:

> I just want to give up.

. . . being confident of this very thing, that He Who has begun a good work in you will complete it until the day of Jesus Christ.
PHILIPPIANS 1:6

Though he fall, he shall not be utterly cast down; for the LORD upholds him with His hand.
PSALM 37:24

. . . who are kept by the power of God through faith for salvation ready to be revealed in the last time.
1 PETER 1:5

And the Lord said, "Simon, Simon! Indeed, Satan has asked for you, that he may sift you as wheat. But I have prayed for you, that your faith should not fail; and when you have returned to Me, strengthen your brethren."
LUKE 22:31–32

. . . looking unto Jesus, the author and finisher of our faith, Who for the joy that was set before Him endured the cross, despising the shame, and has sat down at the right hand of the throne of God. For consider Him Who endured such hostility from sinners against Himself, lest you become weary and discouraged in your souls.
HEBREWS 12:2–3

But he who looks into the perfect law of liberty and continues in it, and is not a forgetful hearer but a doer of the work, this one will be blessed in what he does.
JAMES 1:25

And he who overcomes, and keeps My works until the end, to him I will give power over the nations — He shall rule them with a rod of iron; they shall be dashed to pieces like the potter's vessels — as I also have received from My Father; and I will give him the morning star.
REVELATION 2:26–28

4

MY
HEALTH

THINK THIS:

As a child of Almighty God, I always have hope. He can do the impossible in my life.

NOT THAT:

I have no hope of ever getting well.

But He was wounded for our transgressions, He was bruised for our iniquities; the chastisement for our peace was upon Him, and by His stripes we are healed.
ISAIAH 53:5

But if the Spirit of Him Who raised Jesus from the dead dwells in you, He Who raised Christ from the dead will also give life to your mortal bodies through His Spirit Who dwells in you.
ROMANS 8:11

He sent His word and healed them, and delivered them from their destructions.
PSALM 107:20

My son, give attention to my words; incline your ear to my sayings. Do not let them depart from your eyes; keep them in the midst of your heart; for they are life to those who find them, and health to all their flesh.
PROVERBS 4:20–22

Is anyone among you sick? Let him call for the elders of the church, and let them pray over him,

anointing him with oil in the name of the Lord. And the prayer of faith will save the sick, and the Lord will raise him up. And if he has committed sins, he will be forgiven.
JAMES 5:14–15

Bless the LORD, O my soul, and forget not all His benefits: Who forgives all your iniquities, Who heals all your diseases . . .
PSALM 103:2–3

Then Jesus went about all the cities and villages, teaching in their synagogues, preaching the gospel of the kingdom, and healing every sickness and every disease among the people.
MATTHEW 9:35

Beloved, I pray that you may prosper in all things and be in health, just as your soul prospers.
3 JOHN 1:2

And the whole multitude sought to touch Him, for power went out from Him and healed them all.
LUKE 6:19

THINK THIS:
God has given me wisdom, and
He is guiding my steps.

NOT THAT:
I'm facing such difficult choices;
I don't know what to do.

Show me Your ways, O LORD; teach me Your paths.
Lead me in Your truth and teach me, for You are the
God of my salvation; on You I wait all the day.
PSALM 25:4–5

The secret things belong to the LORD our God, but
those things which are revealed belong to us and to
our children forever, that we may do all the words
of this law.
DEUTERONOMY 29:29

And we know that all things work together for
good to those who love God, to those who are the
called according to His purpose.
ROMANS 8:28

Let us hold fast the confession of our hope without
wavering, for He Who promised is faithful.
HEBREWS 10:23

Many people shall come and say, "Come, and let
us go up to the mountain of the LORD, to the
house of the God of Jacob; He will teach us His
ways, and we shall walk in His paths." For out of

Zion shall go forth the law, and the word of the LORD from Jerusalem.
ISAIAH 2:3

But as it is written: "Eye has not seen, nor ear heard, nor have entered into the heart of man the things which God has prepared for those who love Him." But God has revealed them to us through His Spirit. For the Spirit searches all things, yes, the deep things of God.
1 CORINTHIANS 2:9–10

The LORD will perfect that which concerns me; Your mercy, O LORD, endures forever; do not forsake the works of Your hands.
PSALM 138:8

 **THINK THIS:**

God can do a "suddenly" miracle in my life. His timing is perfect. I trust Him.

 NOT THAT:

I've been sick for so long; it will never end.

I would have lost heart, unless I had believed that I would see the goodness of the LORD in the land of the living. Wait on the LORD; be of good courage, and He shall strengthen your heart; wait, I say, on the LORD!
PSALM 27:13–14

Lead me in Your truth and teach me, for You are the God of my salvation; on You I wait all the day.
PSALM 25:5

I wait for the LORD my soul waits, and in His word I do hope.
PSALM 130:5

This I recall to my mind, therefore I have hope. Through the LORD's mercies we are not consumed, because His compassions fail not. They are new every morning; great is Your faithfulness. "The LORD is my portion," says my soul, "Therefore I hope in Him!" The LORD is good to those who wait for Him, to the soul who seeks Him. It is good that one should hope and wait quietly for the salvation of the LORD.
LAMENTATIONS 3:21–26

Indeed, let no one who waits on You be ashamed; let those be ashamed who deal treacherously without cause. Show me Your ways, O LORD; teach me Your paths.
PSALM 25:3&4

Have you not known? Have you not heard? The everlasting God, the LORD, the Creator of the ends of the earth, neither faints nor is weary. His understanding is unsearchable. He gives power to the weak, and to those who have no might He increases strength. Even the youths shall faint and be weary, and the young men shall utterly

fall, but those who wait on the LORD shall renew their strength; they shall mount up with wings like eagles, they shall run and not be weary, they shall walk and not faint.
ISAIAH 40:28–31

The eyes of all look expectantly to You, and You give them their food in due season. You open Your hand and satisfy the desire of every living thing.
PSALM 145:15–16

Our soul waits for the LORD; He is our help and our shield.
PSALM 33:20

 **THINK THIS:**

> **I am all that God says I am — strong, confident, healthy, victorious, and more than an overcomer.**

 NOT THAT:

> **I feel weak and helpless.**

Yet in all these things we are more than conquerors through Him Who loved us.
ROMANS 8:37

The LORD will guide you continually, and satisfy your soul in drought, and strengthen your bones;

you shall be like a watered garden, and like a spring of water, whose waters do not fail.
ISAIAH 58:11

For You are my rock and my fortress; therefore, for Your name's sake, lead me and guide me.
PSALM 31:3

Thus says the LORD, your Redeemer, the Holy One of Israel: "I am the LORD your God, Who teaches you to profit, Who leads you by the way you should go."
ISAIAH 48:17

The LORD is my shepherd; I shall not want. He makes me to lie down in green pastures; He leads me beside the still waters. He restores my soul; He leads me in the paths of righteousness for His name's sake.
PSALM 23:1–3

Commit your works to the LORD, and your thoughts will be established.
PROVERBS 16:3

However, when He, the Spirit of truth, has come, He will guide you into all truth; for He will not speak on His own authority, but whatever He hears He will speak; and He will tell you things to come.
JOHN 16:13

Your word is a lamp to my feet and a light to my path.
PSALM 119:105

Trust in the LORD with all your heart, and lean not on your own understanding; in all your ways acknowledge Him, and He shall direct your paths.
PROVERBS 3:5–6

Your ears shall hear a word behind you, saying, "This is the way, walk in it," whenever you turn to the right hand or whenever you turn to the left.
ISAIAH 30:21

 **THINK THIS:**

God sees me when I am hurting.
He will never leave me, and He will
surround me with the right people.

 NOT THAT:

No one cares about me or
what I'm going through.

You number my wanderings; put my tears into Your bottle; are they not in Your book?
PSALM 56:8

My soul, wait silently for God alone, for my expectation is from Him. He only is my rock and my salvation;

He is my defense; I shall not be moved. In God is my salvation and my glory; the rock of my strength, and my refuge, is in God.
PSALM 62:5–7

Do not be a terror to me; You are my hope in the day of doom.
JEREMIAH 17:17

Keep me as the apple of Your eye; hide me under the shadow of Your wings . . .
PSALM 17:8

He raises the poor out of the dust, and lifts the needy out of the ash heap, that He may seat him with princes — with the princes of His people. He grants the barren woman a home, like a joyful mother of children. Praise the LORD!
PSALM 113:7–9

When you pass through the waters, I will be with you; and through the rivers, they shall not overflow you. When you walk through the fire, you shall not be burned, nor shall the flame scorch you.
ISAIAH 43:2

For in the time of trouble He shall hide me in His pavilion; in the secret place of His tabernacle He shall hide me; He shall set me high upon a rock.
PSALM 27:5

Yea, though I walk through the valley of the shadow of death, I will fear no evil; for You are with me; Your rod and Your staff, they comfort me.
PSALM 23:4

 *THINK THIS:*

God is the same yesterday, today, and forever. I'm going to stay in faith, standing on His promises of healing.

 NOT THAT:

God used to heal people, but I don't know if I believe He still does.

. . . and He cast out the spirits with a word, and healed all who were sick, that it might be fulfilled which was spoken by Isaiah the prophet, saying: "He Himself took our infirmities and bore our sicknesses."
MATTHEW 8:16–17

Surely He shall deliver you from the snare of the fowler and from the perilous pestilence. He shall cover you with His feathers, and under His wings you shall take refuge; His truth shall be your shield and buckler. You shall not be afraid of the terror by night, nor of the arrow that flies by day, nor of the pestilence that walks in darkness, nor of the destruction that lays waste at noonday. A thousand may fall at your side, and

ten thousand at your right hand; but it shall not come near you.
PSALM 91:3-7

So He came and took her by the hand and lifted her up, and immediately the fever left her. And she served them.
MARK 1:31

And when He had come into the house, the blind men came to Him. And Jesus said to them, "Do you believe that I am able to do this?" They said to Him, "Yes, Lord." Then He touched their eyes, saying, "According to your faith let it be to you."
MATTHEW 9:28-29

Then Jesus said to him, "Go your way; your faith has made you well." And immediately he received his sight and followed Jesus on the road.
MARK 10:52

Surely He has borne our griefs and carried our sorrows; yet we esteemed Him stricken, smitten by God, and afflicted.
ISAIAH 53:4

And one of them, when he saw that he was healed, returned, and with a loud voice glorified God.
LUKE 17:15

But as for me, when they were sick, my clothing was sackcloth; I humbled myself with fasting; and my prayer would return to my own heart.
PSALM 35:13

So he, leaping up, stood and walked and entered the temple with them — walking, leaping, and praising God.
ACTS 3:8

 **THINK THIS:**

My health, my future, and my destiny are in God's hands. He has the final word, and I will trust in Him.

 NOT THAT:

The doctors say there is no hope, and I'm starting to believe them.

Heal me, O LORD, and I shall be healed; save me, and I shall be saved, for You are my praise.
JEREMIAH 17:14

You are the God Who does wonders; You have declared Your strength among the peoples.
PSALM 77:14

For we know that if our earthly house, this tent, is destroyed, we have a building from God, a house not made with hands, eternal in the heavens.
2 CORINTHIANS 5:1

For this is God, our God forever and ever; He will be our guide even to death.
PSALM 48:14

I shall not die, but live, and declare the works of the LORD.
PSALM 118:17

But God will redeem my soul from the power of the grave, for He shall receive me.
PSALM 49:15

Before I was afflicted I went astray, but now I keep Your word. You are good, and do good; teach me Your statutes.
PSALM 119:67–68

While I live I will praise the LORD; I will sing praises to my God while I have my being.
PSALM 146:2

Yea, though I walk through the valley of the shadow of death, I will fear no evil; for You are with me; Your rod and Your staff, they comfort me.
PSALM 23:4

THINK THIS:

God hears me when I cry out to Him, and He is working on my behalf.

NOT THAT:

I pray about my illness, but I don't know if God even hears me.

Now this is the confidence that we have in Him, that if we ask anything according to His will, He hears us. And if we know that He hears us, whatever we ask, we know that we have the petitions that we have asked of Him.
1 JOHN 5:14–15

For with God nothing will be impossible.
LUKE 1:37

Let us hold fast the confession of our hope without wavering, for He Who promised is faithful.
HEBREWS 10:23

If you diligently heed the voice of the LORD your God and do what is right in His sight, give ear to His commandments and keep all His statutes, I will put none of the diseases on you which I have brought on the Egyptians. For I am the LORD Who heals you.
EXODUS 15:26

. . . that you do not become sluggish, but imitate those who through faith and patience inherit the promises.
HEBREWS 6:12

Now faith is the substance of things hoped for, the evidence of things not seen.
HEBREWS 11:1

. . . by which have been given to us exceedingly great and precious promises, that through these you may be partakers of the divine nature, having escaped the corruption that is in the world through lust. But also for this very reason, giving all diligence, add to your faith virtue, to virtue knowledge, to knowledge self-control, to self-control perseverance, to perseverance godliness, to godliness brotherly kindness, and to brotherly kindness love. For if these things are yours and abound, you will be neither barren nor unfruitful in the knowledge of our Lord Jesus Christ.
2 PETER 1:4–8

But without faith it is impossible to please Him, for he who comes to God must believe that He is, and that He is a rewarder of those who diligently seek Him.
HEBREWS 11:6

Concerning this thing I pleaded with the Lord three times that it might depart from me. And He said to me, "My grace is sufficient for you, for My strength is made perfect in weakness." Therefore most gladly I will rather boast in my infirmities, that the power of Christ may rest upon me.
2 CORINTHIANS 12:8–9

 **THINK THIS:**

I don't have to earn God's goodness. He loves me unconditionally, and He will make all things work together for good in my life.

 NOT THAT:

I've been trying to do right. Why are bad things happening to me?

Yes, I have loved you with an everlasting love; Therefore with lovingkindness I have drawn you.
JEREMIAH 31:3

And of His fullness we have all received, and grace for grace. For the law was given through Moses, but grace and truth came through Jesus Christ.
JOHN 1:16–17

Beloved, do not think it strange concerning the fiery trial which is to try you, as though some strange thing happened to you; but rejoice to the extent that you partake of Christ's sufferings, that when His glory is revealed, you may also be glad with exceeding joy.
1 PETER 4:12–13

Cast your burden on the LORD, and He shall sustain you; He shall never permit the righteous to be moved.
PSALM 55:22

But, beloved, do not forget this one thing, that with the Lord one day is as a thousand years, and a thousand years as one day. The Lord is not slack concerning His promise, as some count slackness, but is longsuffering toward us, not willing that any should perish but that all should come to repentance.

2 PETER 3:8–9

Why are you cast down, O my soul? And why are you disquieted within me? Hope in God; for I shall yet praise Him, the help of my countenance and my God.

PSALM 43:5

Hear me, O LORD, for Your lovingkindness is good; turn to me according to the multitude of Your tender mercies. And do not hide Your face from Your servant, for I am in trouble; hear me speedily. Draw near to my soul, and redeem it; deliver me because of my enemies.

PSALM 69:16–18

THINK THIS:

No matter how I feel, I am going to praise God and declare His faithfulness over me and my loved ones.

NOT THAT:

I find myself complaining all the time because of my sickness.

Therefore by Him let us continually offer the sacrifice of praise to God, that is, the fruit of our lips, giving thanks to His name.
HEBREWS 13:15

And when he had consulted with the people, he appointed those who should sing to the LORD, and who should praise the beauty of holiness, as they went out before the army and were saying: "Praise the LORD, for His mercy endures forever."
2 CHRONICLES 20:21

Worthy is the Lamb Who was slain to receive power and riches and wisdom, and strength and honor and glory and blessing!
REVELATION 5:12

You who fear the LORD, praise Him! All you descendants of Jacob, glorify Him, and fear Him, all you offspring of Israel!
PSALM 22:23

Oh, that men would give thanks to the LORD for His goodness, and for His wonderful works to the children of men!
PSALM 107:8

Oh, sing to the LORD a new song! Sing to the LORD, all the earth.
PSALM 96:1

Daniel answered and said: "Blessed be the name of God forever and ever, for wisdom and might are His."
DANIEL 2:20

O LORD, You are my God. I will exalt You, I will praise Your name, for You have done wonderful things; Your counsels of old are faithfulness and truth.
ISAIAH 25:1

Blessed be the God and Father of our Lord Jesus Christ, Who according to His abundant mercy has begotten us again to a living hope through the resurrection of Jesus Christ from the dead, to an inheritance incorruptible and undefiled and that does not fade away, reserved in heaven for you.
1 PETER 1:3–4

5

MY RELATIONSHIP WITH GOD

THINK THIS:

I am a child of God, saved by grace
through faith in Jesus. Nothing or no
one can ever take that from me.

NOT THAT:

Am I really saved?

My sheep hear My voice, and I know them, and they
follow Me. And I give them eternal life, and they shall
never perish; neither shall anyone snatch them out
of My hand.
JOHN 10:27–28

And we know that the Son of God has come and has
given us an understanding, that we may know Him
Who is true; and we are in Him Who is true, in His Son
Jesus Christ. This is the true God and eternal life.
1 JOHN 5:20

I am the resurrection and the life. He who believes
in Me, though he may die, he shall live. And whoever lives and believes in Me shall never die.
JOHN 11:25–26

And this is eternal life, that they may know You,
the only true God, and Jesus Christ Whom You
have sent.
JOHN 17:3

Do not labor for the food which perishes, but for
the food which endures to everlasting life, which

the Son of Man will give you, because God the Father has set His seal on Him.
JOHN 6:27

And this is the testimony; that God has given to us eternal life, and this life is in His Son.
1 JOHN 5:11

Fight the good fight of faith, lay hold on eternal life, to which you were also called . . .
1 TIMOTHY 6:12

But God will redeem my soul from the power of the grave, for He shall receive me.
PSALM 49:15

So when this corruptible has put on incorruption, and this mortal has put on immortality, then shall be brought to pass the saying that is written: "Death is swallowed up in victory." O Death, where is your sting? O Hades, where is your victory?
1 CORINTHIANS 15:54–55

These things I have written to you who believe in the name of the Son of God, that you may know that you have eternal life, and that you may continue to believe in the name of the Son of God.
1 JOHN 5:13

Most assuredly, I say to you, he who hears My word and believes in Him Who sent Me has everlasting

life, and shall not come into judgment, but has passed from death into life.
JOHN 5:24

For God so loved the world that He gave His only begotten Son, that whoever believes in Him should not perish but have everlasting life.
JOHN 3:16

THINK THIS:
I can trust that God will keep His promises, doing exceedingly abundantly more than I can even imagine.

NOT THAT:
I'm not sure if I can really rely on what God says.

All Scripture is given by inspiration of God, and is profitable for doctrine, for reproof, for correction, for instruction in righteousness, that the man of God may be complete, thoroughly equipped for every good work.
2 TIMOTHY 3:16–17

Your word I have hidden in my heart, that I might not sin against You.
PSALM 119:11

This Book of the Law shall not depart from your mouth, but you shall meditate in it day and night, that you may observe to do according to all that is written in it. For then you will make your way prosperous, and then you will have good success.
JOSHUA 1:8

Now to Him Who is able to do exceedingly abundantly above all that we ask or think, according to the power that works in us, to Him be glory in the church by Christ Jesus to all generations, forever and ever. Amen.
EPHESIANS 3:20–21

Forever, O LORD, Your word is settled in heaven.
PSALM 119:89

Then Jesus said to those Jews who believed Him, "If you abide in My word, you are My disciples indeed. And you shall know the truth, and the truth shall make you free."
JOHN 8:31–32

Your testimonies also are my delight and my counselors.
PSALM 119:24

So He humbled you, allowed you to hunger, and fed you with manna which you did not know nor did your fathers know, that He might make you know that man shall not live by bread alone; but man

lives by every word that proceeds from the mouth of the LORD.
DEUTERONOMY 8:3

 **THINK THIS:**
God knows what is best for my life, and I take joy in obeying His Word.

 NOT THAT:
Is it really worth it to obey God?

But whoever keeps His word, truly the love of God is perfected in him. By this we know that we are in Him. He who says he abides in Him ought himself also to walk just as He walked.
1 JOHN 2:5–6

Therefore you shall keep every commandment which I command you today, that you may be strong, and go in and possess the land which you cross over to possess, and that you may prolong your days in the land which the LORD swore to give your fathers, to them and their descendants, a land flowing with milk and honey.
DEUTERONOMY 11:8&9

So if you walk in My ways, to keep My statutes and My commandments, as your father David walked, then I will lengthen your days.
1 KINGS 3:14

Teach me to do Your will, for You are my God; Your Spirit is good. Lead me in the land of uprightness.
PSALM 143:10

Obey My voice, and I will be your God, and you shall be My people. And walk in all the ways that I have commanded you, that it may be well with you.
JEREMIAH 7:23

Oh, that you had heeded My commandments! Then your peace would have been like a river, and your righteousness like the waves of the sea.
ISAIAH 48:18

He who has My commandments and keeps them, it is he who loves Me. And he who loves Me will be loved by My Father, and I will love him and manifest Myself to him.
JOHN 14:21

Behold, I set before you today a blessing and a curse: the blessing, if you obey the commandments of the LORD your God which I command you today; and the curse, if you do not obey the commandments of the LORD your God, but turn aside from the way which I command you today, to go after other gods which you have not known.
DEUTERONOMY 11:26–28

If you love Me, keep My commandments.
JOHN 14:15

 **THINK THIS:**
The fear of the Lord is trusting God's plan for my life and living according to His Word. It's the best way to live.

 NOT THAT:
I can do whatever I want.

Let us hear the conclusion of the whole matter: fear God and keep His commandments, for this is man's all. For God will bring every work into judgment, including every secret thing, whether good or evil.
ECCLESIASTES 12:13–14

In mercy and truth atonement is provided for iniquity; and by the fear of the LORD one departs from evil.
PROVERBS 16:6

He does not delight in the strength of the horse; He takes no pleasure in the legs of a man. The LORD takes pleasure in those who fear Him, in those who hope in His mercy.
PSALM 147:10–11

And to man He said, "Behold, the fear of the Lord, that is wisdom, and to depart from evil is understanding."
JOB 28:28

If you seek her as silver, and search for her as for hidden treasures; then you will understand the fear of the LORD, and find the knowledge of God.
PROVERBS 2:4–5

In the fear of the LORD there is strong confidence, and His children will have a place of refuge. The fear of the LORD is a fountain of life, to turn one away from the snares of death.
PROVERBS 14:26–27

Praise the LORD! Blessed is the man who fears the LORD, who delights greatly in His commandments.
PSALM 112:1

Who is the man that fears the LORD? Him shall He teach in the way He chooses. He himself shall dwell in prosperity, and his descendants shall inherit the earth. The secret of the LORD is with those who fear Him, and He will show them His covenant.
PSALM 25:12–14

The fear of the LORD is the beginning of knowledge, but fools despise wisdom and instruction.
PROVERBS 1:7

The fear of the LORD leads to life, and he who has it will abide in satisfaction; He will not be visited with evil.
PROVERBS 19:23

THINK THIS:

Breakthroughs are coming in my life, sudden bursts of God's goodness. He will provide everything I need and more.

NOT THAT:

I know God can meet my needs, but I'm not sure He will.

Trust in the LORD, and do good; dwell in the land, and feed on His faithfulness. Delight yourself also in the LORD, and He shall give you the desires of your heart.
PSALM 37:3–4

I will sing of the mercies of the LORD forever; with my mouth will I make known Your faithfulness to all generations. For I have said, "Mercy shall be built up forever: Your faithfulness You shall establish in the very heavens."
PSALM 89:1–2

He is God, the faithful God Who keeps covenant and mercy for a thousand generations with those who love Him and keep His commandments.
DEUTERONOMY 7:9

Behold, I am with you and will keep you wherever you go, and will bring you back to this land; for I will not leave you until I have done what I have spoken to you.
GENESIS 28:15

Not one thing has failed of all the good things which the LORD your God spoke concerning you. All have come to pass for you; not one word of them has failed.
JOSHUA 23:14

If we are faithless, He remains faithful; He cannot deny Himself.
2 TIMOTHY 2:13

"For the mountains shall depart and the hills be removed, but My kindness shall not depart from you, nor shall My covenant of peace be removed," says the LORD, Who has mercy on you.
ISAIAH 54:10

Your faithfulness endures to all generations . . .
PSALM 119:90

This I recall to my mind, there I have hope. Through the LORD's mercies we are not consumed, because His compassions fail not. They are new every morning; great is Your faithfulness.
LAMENTATIONS 3:21–23

He Who calls you is faithful, Who also will do it.
1 THESSALONIANS 5:24

He will not allow your foot to be moved; He Who keeps you will not slumber. Behold, He Who keeps Israel shall neither slumber nor sleep.
PSALM 121:3–4

THINK THIS:

My own strength may fail, but God will never fail me. He is the source of all good things in my life.

NOT THAT:

I've got my life figured out pretty well on my own.

For whoever exalts himself will be humbled, and he who humbles himself will be exalted.
LUKE 14:11

Come now, you who say, "Today or tomorrow we will go to such and such a city, spend a year there, buy and sell, and make a profit"; whereas you do not know what will happen tomorrow. For what is your life? It is even a vapor that appears for a little time and then vanishes away. Instead you ought to say, "If the Lord wills, we shall live and do this or that." But now you boast in your arrogance. All such boasting is evil.
JAMES 4:13–16

The way of a fool is right in his own eyes, but he who heeds counsel is wise.
PROVERBS 12:15

LORD, my heart is not haughty, nor my eyes lofty. Neither do I concern myself with great matters, nor with things too profound for me.
PSALM 131:1

Therefore humble yourselves under the mighty hand of God, that He may exalt you in due time.
1 PETER 5:6

But He gives more grace. Therefore He says: "God resists the proud, but gives grace to the humble."
JAMES 4:6

If My people who are called by My name will humble themselves, and pray and see My face, and turn from their wicked ways, then I will hear from heaven, and will forgive their sin and heal their land.
2 CHRONICLES 7:14

 **THINK THIS:**
I am forgiven, redeemed, and restored.
My past doesn't define me. My best
days are still out ahead of me.

 NOT THAT:
What I've done is too bad for
God to ever use me.

Let us therefore come boldly to the throne of grace, that we may obtain mercy and find grace to help in time of need.
HEBREWS 4:16

For by grace you have been saved through faith, and that not of yourselves; it is the gift of God, not of works, lest anyone should boast. For we are His workmanship, created in Christ Jesus for good works, which God prepared beforehand that we should walk in them.
EPHESIANS 2:8–10

By the grace of God I am what I am, and His grace toward me was not in vain; but I labored more abundantly than they all, yet not I, but the grace of God which was with me.
1 CORINTHIANS 15:10

And of His fullness we have all received, and grace for grace. For the law was given through Moses, but grace and truth came through Jesus Christ.
JOHN 1:16–17

We ourselves were also once foolish, disobedient, deceived, serving various lusts and pleasures, living in malice and envy, hateful and hating one another. But when the kindness and the love of God our Savior toward man appeared, not by works of righteousness which we have done, according to his mercy He saved us, through the washing of regeneration and renewing of the Holy Spirit, Whom He poured out on us abundantly through Jesus Christ our Savior, that having been justified by His grace we should become heirs according to the hope of eternal life.
TITUS 3:3–7

You have found grace in My sight, and I know you by name.

EXODUS 33:17

For you know the grace of our Lord Jesus Christ, that though He was rich, yet for your sakes He became poor, that you through His poverty might become rich.

2 CORINTHIANS 8:9

. . . to the praise of the glory of His grace, by which He made us accepted in the Beloved.

EPHESIANS 1:6

For the grace of God that brings salvation has appeared to all men, teaching us that, denying ungodliness and worldly lusts, we should live soberly, righteously, and godly in the present age, looking for the blessed hope and glorious appearing of our great God and Savior Jesus Christ, Who gave Himself for us, that He might redeem us from every lawless deed and purify for Himself His own special people zealous for good works.

TITUS 2:11–14

THINK THIS:

God is doing His perfect work in me. I never have to go back to my old life. He is making all things.

NOT THAT:

I'm going to fall back into old habits and addictions.

For you were once darkness, but now you are light in the Lord. Walk as children of light.
EPHESIANS 5:8

For I am the LORD Who brings you up out of the land of Egypt, to be your God. You shall therefore be holy, for I am holy.
LEVITICUS 11:45

Therefore, as the elect of God, holy and beloved, put on tender mercies, kindness, humility, meekness, longsuffering.
COLOSSIANS 3:12

Pursue peace with all people, and holiness, without which no one will see the Lord.
HEBREWS 12:14

. . . Who has saved us and called us with a holy calling, not according to our works, but according to His own purpose and grace which was given to us in Christ Jesus before time began.
2 TIMOTHY 1:9

Sanctify them by Your truth. Your word is truth.
JOHN 17:17

For to this you were called, because Christ also suffered for us, leaving us an example, that you should follow His steps: Who committed no sin, nor was deceit found in His mouth.
1 PETER 2:21–22

I beseech you therefore, brethren, by the mercies of God, that you present your bodies a living sacrifice, holy, acceptable to God, which is your reasonable service.
ROMANS 12:1

For God did not call us to uncleanness, but in holiness.
1 THESSALONIANS 4:7

 *THINK THIS:*

I am a child of Almighty God with royal DNA running through my veins. He is a perfect Father Who loves me unconditionally.

 NOT THAT:

I don't see how God could love me.

Yes, I have loved you with an everlasting love; therefore with lovingkindness I have drawn you.
JEREMIAH 31:3

In this is love, not that we loved God, but that He loved us and sent His Son to be the propitiation for our sins. Beloved, if God so loved us, we also ought to love one another.

1 JOHN 4:10–11

But God, Who is rich in mercy, because of His great love with which He loved us, even when we were dead in trespasses, made us alive together with Christ (by grace you have been saved), and raised us up together, and made us sit together in the heavenly places in Christ Jesus, that in the ages to come He might show the exceeding riches of His grace in His kindness toward us in Christ Jesus.

EPHESIANS 2:4–7

For I am persuaded that neither death nor life, nor angels nor principalities nor powers, nor things present nor things to come, nor height nor depth, nor any other created thing, shall be able to separate us from the love of God which is in Christ Jesus our Lord.

ROMANS 8:38–39

As the Father loved Me, I also have loved you; abide in My love. If you keep My commandments, you will abide in My love, just as I have kept My Father's commandments and abide in His love.

JOHN 15:9–10

Greater love has no one than this, than to lay down one's life for his friends.
JOHN 15:13

A new commandment I give to you, that you love one another; as I have loved you, that you also love one another. By this all will know that you are My disciples, if you have love for one another.
JOHN 13:34–35

Beloved, let us love one another, for love is of God; and everyone who loves is born of God and knows God. He who does not love does not know God, for God is love.
1 JOHN 4:7–8

THINK THIS:
I'm not called to just survive; I will thrive. God has a life of peace, favor, strength, accomplishment, and joy in store for me.

NOT THAT:
I hear people talking about enjoying God, but it isn't that way for me.

Now acquaint yourself with Him, and be at peace; thereby good will come to you.
JOB 22:21

Indeed My hand has laid the foundation of the earth, and My right hand has stretched out the heavens; when I call to them, they stand up together. All of you, assemble yourselves, and hear! Who among them has declared these things? The LORD loves him; He shall do His pleasure on Babylon, and His arm shall be against the Chaldeans.
ISAIAH 48:13–14

Delight yourself also in the LORD, and He shall give you the desires of your heart.
PSALM 37:4

But his delight is in the law of the LORD, and in His law he meditates day and night.
PSALM 1:2

Praise the LORD! Blessed is the man who fears the LORD, who delights greatly in His commandments.
PSALM 112:1

In the multitude of my anxieties within me, Your comforts delight my soul.
PSALM 94:19

Your testimonies also are my delight and my counselors.
PSALM 119:24

And they took strong cities and a rich land, and possessed houses full of all goods, cisterns already dug, vineyards, olive groves, and fruit trees in abun-

dance. So they ate and were filled and grew fat, and delighted themselves in Your great goodness.
NEHEMIAH 9:25

 *THINK THIS:*

> Because God cares for me, His love, favor, and blessing are lightening the load and paving the way for me.

 NOT THAT:

> I'm not sure that I can trust God to care about me.

But God demonstrates His own love toward us, in that while we were still sinners, Christ died for us.
ROMANS 5:8

For God so loved the world that He gave His only begotten Son, that whoever believes in Him should not perish but have everlasting life.
JOHN 3:16

And we have known and believed the love that God has for us. God is love, and he who abides in love abides in God, and God in him.
1 JOHN 4:16

Behold what manner of love the Father has bestowed on us, that we should be called children of God! Therefore the world does not know us, because it did not know Him.

1 JOHN 3:1

And this is His commandment: that we should believe on the name of His Son Jesus Christ and love one another, as He gave us commandment.

1 JOHN 3:23

So Jesus answered and said to them, "Have faith in God."

MARK 11:22

Simon Peter, a bondservant and apostle of Jesus Christ, to those who have obtained like precious faith with us by the righteousness of our God and Savior Jesus Christ.

2 PETER 1:1

. . . through Whom also we have access by faith into this grace in which we stand, and rejoice in hope of the glory of God.

ROMANS 5:2

 **THINK THIS:**
I submit my life to God's Word
and His purposes for me.

 NOT THAT:
I want to make my decisions and
do things my own way.

Commit your works to the LORD, and your thoughts
will be established.
PROVERBS 16:3

Therefore submit to God. Resist the devil and he
will flee from you.
JAMES 4:7

"If you are willing and obedient, you shall eat the
good of the land; but if you refuse and rebel, you
shall be devoured by the sword"; for the mouth
of the LORD has spoken.
ISAIAH 1:19–20

Let this mind be in you which was also in Christ
Jesus, Who, being in the form of God, did not consider it robbery to be equal with God, but made
Himself of no reputation, taking the form of a
bondservant, and coming in the likeness of men.
And being found in appearance as a man, He humbled Himself and became obedient to the point of
death, even the death of the cross.
PHILIPPIANS 2:5–8

Trust in the LORD with all your heart, and lean not on your own understanding; In all your ways acknowledge Him, and He shall direct your paths.
PROVERBS 3:5–6

Therefore gird up the loins of your mind, be sober, and rest your hope fully upon the grace that is to be brought to you at the revelation of Jesus Christ; as obedient children, not conforming yourselves to the former lusts, as in your ignorance.
1 PETER 1:13–14

So Samuel said: "Has the LORD as great delight in burnt offerings and sacrifices, as in obeying the voice of the LORD? Behold, to obey is better than sacrifice, and to heed than the fat of rams. For rebellion is as the sin of witchcraft, and stubbornness is as iniquity and idolatry. Because you have rejected the word of the LORD, He also has rejected you from being king."
1 SAMUEL 15:22–23

 THINK THIS:

God is the strength of my life. I can bring any trouble or problem to Him. He will make all things work together for my good.

 NOT THAT:

I don't know where to turn with my problems.

I will be glad and rejoice in Your mercy, for You have considered my trouble; You have known my soul in adversities.

PSALM 31:7

I will lift up my eyes to the hills — from when comes my help? My help comes from the LORD, Who made heaven and earth.

PSALM 121:1

The LORD builds up Jerusalem; He gathers together the outcasts of Israel. He heals the brokenhearted and binds up their wounds. He counts the number of the stars; He calls them all by name. Great is our Lord, and mighty in power; His understanding is infinite. The LORD lifts up the humble; He casts the wicked down to the ground.

PSALM 147:2–6

Peace I leave with you, My peace I give to you; not as the world gives do I give to you. Let not your heart be troubled, neither let it be afraid.

JOHN 14:27

Turn Yourself to me, and have mercy on me, for I am desolate and afflicted. The troubles of my heart have enlarged; bring me out of my distresses! Look on my affliction and my pain, and forgive all my sins.

PSALM 25:16–18

I will bless the LORD at all times; His praise shall continually be in my mouth. My soul shall make its boast in the LORD; the humble shall hear of it and be glad. Oh, magnify the LORD with me, and let us exalt His name together. I sought the LORD, and He heard me, and delivered me from all my fears. They looked to Him and were radiant, and their faces were not ashamed. This poor man cried out, and the LORD heard him, and saved him out of all his troubles. The angel of the LORD encamps all around those who fear Him, and delivers them. Oh, taste and see that the LORD is good; blessed is the man who trusts in Him!

PSALM 34:1-8

THINK THIS:

I am an overcomer in Christ Jesus, equipped and empowered to break any chain or stronghold that would try to hold me back from God's best.

NOT THAT:

I'll never overcome this struggle with sin in my life.

Stand fast therefore in the liberty by which Christ has made us free, and do not be entangled again with a yoke of bondage.

GALATIANS 5:1

Create in me a clean heart, O God, and renew a steadfast spirit within me.
PSALM 51:10

Wash yourselves, make yourselves clean; put away the evil of your doings from before My eyes. Cease to do evil, learn to do good; seek justice, rebuke the oppressor; defend the fatherless, plead for the widow. "Come now, and let us reason together," says the LORD, "Though your sins are like scarlet, they shall be as white as snow; though they are red like crimson, they shall be as wool. If you are willing and obedient, you shall eat the good of the land."
ISAIAH 1:16–19

I have been crucified with Christ; it is no longer I who live, but Christ lives in me; and the life which I now live in the flesh I live by faith in the Son of God, Who loved me and gave Himself for me.
GALATIANS 2:20

Therefore, if anyone is in Christ, he is a new creation; old things have passed away; behold, all things have become new. Now all things are of God, Who has reconciled us to Himself through Jesus Christ, and has given us the ministry of reconciliation, that is, that God was in Christ reconciling the world to Himself, not imputing their trespasses to them, and has committed to us the word of reconciliation. Now then, we are ambassadors for Christ, as though God were pleading

through us: we implore you on Christ's behalf, be reconciled to God. For He made Him Who knew no sin to be sin for us, that we might become the righteousness of God in Him.
2 CORINTHIANS 5:17–21

This is the message which we have heard from Him and declare to you, that God is light and in Him is no darkness at all. If we say that we have fellowship with Him, and walk in darkness, we lie and do not practice the truth. But if we walk in the light as He is in the light, we have fellowship with one another, and the blood of Jesus Christ His Son cleanses us from all sin. If we say that we have no sin, we deceive ourselves, and the truth is not in us. If we confess our sins, He is faithful and just to forgive us our sins and to cleanse us from all unrighteousness. If we say that we have not sinned, we make Him a liar, and His word is not in us.
1 JOHN 1:5–10

I have taught you in the way of wisdom; I have led you in right paths.
PROVERBS 4:11

THINK THIS:
God is fighting my battles for me.
He will defeat every enemy. I am
destined to live in victory.

NOT THAT:
It feels like the attacks of the
enemy are too strong for me.

For You have been a shelter for me, a strong tower
from the enemy.
PSALM 61:3

If God is for us, who can be against us?
ROMANS 8:31

And they overcame him [Satan] by the blood of the
Lamb and by the word of their testimony, and they
did not love their lives to the death.
REVELATION 12:11

Therefore submit to God. Resist the devil and he
will flee from you.
JAMES 4:7

Then the seventy returned with joy, saying, "Lord,
even the demons are subject to us in Your name."
And He said to them, "I saw Satan fall like lightning
from heaven. Behold, I give you authority to trample
on serpents and scorpions, and over all the power of
the enemy, and nothing shall by any means hurt you."
LUKE 10:17–19

Having disarmed principalities and powers, He made a public spectacle of them, triumphing over them in it.
COLOSSIANS 2:15

Be sober, be vigilant; because your adversary the devil walks about like a roaring lion, seeking whom he may devour. Resist him, steadfast in the faith, knowing that the same sufferings are experienced by brotherhood in the world.
1 PETER 5:8–9

You are of God, little children, and have overcome them, because He Who is in you is greater than he who is in the world.
1 JOHN 4:4

Finally, my brethren, be strong in the LORD and in the power of His might. Put on the whole armor of God, that you may be able to stand against the wiles of the devil. For we do not wrestle against flesh and blood, but against principalities, and against powers, against the rulers of the darkness of this age, against spiritual hosts of wickedness in the heavenly places.
EPHESIANS 6:10–12

He who sins is of the devil, for the devil has sinned from the beginning. For this purpose the Son of God was manifested, that He might destroy the works of the devil.
1 JOHN 3:8

THINK THIS:
I choose to be thankful for the
many blessings in my life.

NOT THAT:
I don't feel satisfied. Why can't I have
the same things others have?

It is good to give thanks to the LORD, and to sing
praises to Your name, O Most High.
PSALM 92:1

Offer to God thanksgiving, and pay your vows to
the Most High.
PSALM 50:14

Be anxious for nothing, but in everything by prayer
and supplication, with thanksgiving, let your requests
be made known to God.
PHILIPPIANS 4:6

And I thank Christ Jesus our Lord Who has enabled
me . . .
1 TIMOTHY 1:12

. . . giving thanks always for all things to God the
Father in the name of our Lord Jesus Christ.
EPHESIANS 5:20

Now when Daniel knew that the writing was signed,
he went home. And in his upper room, with his windows open toward Jerusalem, he knelt down on his

knees three times that day, and prayed and gave thanks before his God, as was his custom since early days.
DANIEL 6:10

So I brought the leaders of Judah up on the wall, and appointed two large thanksgiving choirs.
NEHEMIAH 12:31

We give thanks to God always for you all, making mention of you in our prayers.
1 THESSALONIANS 1:2

Sing praise to the LORD, you saints of His, and give thanks at the remembrance of His holy name.
PSALM 30:4

Oh, give thanks to the LORD, for He is good! For His mercy endures forever. Oh, give thanks to the God of gods! For His mercy endures forever. Oh, give thanks to the Lord of lords! For His mercy endures forever.
PSALM 136:1–3

But thanks be to God, Who gives us the victory through our Lord Jesus Christ.
1 CORINTHIANS 15:57

 **THINK THIS:**

> With God's help, I will rise above every temptation that would try to keep me from choosing His best plan for me.

 NOT THAT:

> This temptation is too strong for me to resist.

For we do not have a High Priest Who cannot sympathize with our weaknesses, but was in all points tempted as we are, yet without sin. Let us therefore come boldly to the throne of grace, that we may obtain mercy and find grace to help in time of need.
HEBREWS 4:15–16

You are of God, little children, and have overcome them, because He Who is in you is greater than he who is in the world.
1 JOHN 4:4

Let no one say when he is tempted, "I am tempted by God"; for God cannot be tempted by evil, nor does He Himself tempt anyone. But each one is tempted when he is drawn away by his own desires and enticed.
JAMES 1:13–14

. . . above all, taking the shield of faith with which you will be able to quench all the fiery darts of the wicked one.
EPHESIANS 6:16

He who covers his sins will not prosper, but whoever confesses and forsakes them will have mercy.
PROVERBS 28:13

Therefore submit to God. Resist the devil and he
will flee from you.
JAMES 4:7

For in that He Himself has suffered, being tempted,
He is able to aid those who are tempted.
HEBREWS 2:18

Your word I have hidden in my heart, that I might
not sin against You.
PSALM 119:11

Now to Him Who is able to keep you from stumbling, and to present you faultless before the
presence of His glory with exceeding joy, to God
our Savior, Who alone is wise, be glory and majesty,
dominion and power, both now and forever. Amen.
JUDE 24–25

 **THINK THIS:**

My relationship with my Heavenly Father
is the most important thing in my life.
I choose to put my trust in Him.

 NOT THAT:

I just don't care about spiritual
things like I used to.

"Yet from the days of your fathers you have gone
away from My ordinances and have not kept them.
Return to Me, and I will return to you," says the LORD
of hosts. "But you said, 'In what way shall we return?'"
MALACHI 3:7

Thus says the LORD: "Stand in the ways and see,
and ask for the old paths, where the good way
is, and walk in it; then you will find rest for your
souls . . ."
JEREMIAH 6:16

Sow for yourselves righteousness; reap in
mercy; break up your fallow ground, for it is time
to seek the LORD, till He comes and rains righteousness on you.
HOSEA 10:12

Beware, brethren, lest there be in any of you an
evil heart of unbelief in departing from the living God; but exhort one another daily, while
it is called "Today," lest any of you be hardened
through the deceitfulness of sin. For we have

become partakers of Christ if we hold the beginning of our confidence steadfast to the end.
HEBREWS 3:12–14

The backslider in heart will be filled with his own ways, but a good man will be satisfied from above.
PROVERBS 14:14

As many as I love, I rebuke and chasten. Therefore be zealous and repent. Behold, I stand at the door and knock. If anyone hears My voice and opens the door, I will come in to him and dine with him, and he with Me. To him who overcomes I will grant to sit with Me on My throne, as I also overcame and sat down with My Father on His throne. "He who has an ear, let him hear what the Spirit says to the churches."
REVELATION 3:19–22

 THINK THIS:

God is not holding my sin against me. He has forgiven me, and He remembers my sins no more.

 NOT THAT:

I still feel guilty for past mistakes, even though I've asked God to forgive me.

Blessed is he whose transgression is forgiven, whose sin is covered. Blessed is the man to whom

the LORD does not impute iniquity, and in whose spirit there is no deceit.
PSALM 32:1-2

You have forgiven the iniquity of Your people; You have covered all their sin.
PSALM 85:2

As far as the east is from the west, so far has He removed our transgressions from us.
PSALM 103:12

Or do you despise the riches of His goodness, forbearance, and longsuffering, not knowing that the goodness of God leads you to repentance?
ROMANS 2:4

And you, being dead in your trespasses and the uncircumcision of your flesh, He has made alive together with Him, having forgiven you all trespasses.
COLOSSIANS 2:13

But I have trusted in Your mercy; my heart shall rejoice in Your salvation. I will sing to the LORD, because He has dealt bountifully with me.
PSALM 13:5-6

"Come now, and let us reason together," says the LORD, "Though your sins are like scarlet, they shall be as white as snow; though they are red like crimson, they shall be as wool."
ISAIAH 1:18

He will again have compassion on us, and will subdue our iniquities. You will cast all our sins into the depths of the sea.
MICAH 7:19

Therefore, if anyone is in Christ, he is a new creation; old things have passed away; behold, all things have become new.
2 CORINTHIANS 5:17

I will cleanse them from all their iniquity by which they have sinned against Me, and I will pardon all their iniquities by which they have sinned and by which they have transgressed against Me.
JEREMIAH 33:8

In Him we have redemption through His blood, the forgiveness of sins, according to the riches of His grace.
EPHESIANS 1:7

If we confess our sins, He is faithful and just to forgive us our sins and to cleanse us from all unrighteousness.
1 JOHN 1:9

Let the wicked forsake his way, and the unrighteous man his thoughts; let him return to the LORD, and He will have mercy on him; and to our God, for He will abundantly pardon.
ISAIAH 55:7

Bless the LORD, O my soul, and forget not all His benefits: Who forgives all your iniquities, Who heals all your diseases, Who redeems your life from destruction, Who crowns you with loving-kindness and tender mercies, Who satisfies your mouth with good things, so that your youth is renewed like the eagle's.
PSALM 103:2–5

 **THINK THIS:**

Not only does God hear my prayer, but He is already making a way for me. I may not see it yet, but I'm going to stay in faith, trusting His promises.

 **NOT THAT:**

I pray and pray, but God doesn't seem to hear.

142

And whatever you ask in My name, that I will do, that the Father may be glorified in the Son.
JOHN 14:13

And whatever things you ask in prayer, believing, you will receive.
MATTHEW 21:22

If you abide in Me, and My words abide in you, you will ask what you desire, and it shall be done for you.
JOHN 15:7

Call to Me, and I will answer you, and show you great and mighty things, which you do not know.
JEREMIAH 33:3

The LORD is near to all who call upon Him, to all who call upon Him in truth. He will fulfill the desire of those who fear Him; He also will hear their cry and save them.
PSALM 145:18–19

And whatever we ask we receive from Him, because we keep His commandments and do those things that are pleasing in His sight.
1 JOHN 3:22

Now this is the confidence that we have in Him, that if we ask anything according to His will, He hears us. And if we know that He hears us, whatever we ask, we know that we have the petitions that we have asked of Him.
1 JOHN 5:14–15

Again I say to you that if two of you agree on earth concerning anything that they ask, it will be done for them by My Father in heaven.
MATTHEW 18:19

Ask, and it will be given to you; seek, and you will find; knock, and it will be opened to you. For everyone who asks receives, and he who seeks finds, and to him who knocks it will be opened. Or what man is there among you who, if his son asks for bread, will give him a stone? Or if he asks for a fish, will he give him a serpent? If you then, being evil, know how to give good gifts to your children, how much more will your Father Who is in heaven give good things to those who ask Him!

MATTHEW 7:7–11

Delight yourself also in the LORD, and He shall give you the desires of your heart.

PSALM 37:4

Then He spoke a parable to them, that men always ought to pray and not lose heart.

LUKE 18:1

 THINK THIS:

I have God's supernatural favor over my life. Supernatural opportunities, healing, restoration, and breakthroughs are coming my way.

 NOT THAT:

I just don't feel like God is doing right by me.

Great is the LORD, and greatly to be praised in the city of our God, in His holy mountain.

PSALM 48:1

Praise the LORD! Sing to the LORD a new song, and His praise in the assembly of saints.
PSALM 149:1

Praise the LORD! Praise, O servants of the LORD, praise the name of the LORD! Blessed be the name of the LORD from this time forth and forevermore! From the rising of the sun to its going down the LORD's name is to be praised.
PSALM 113:1–3

Every good gift and every perfect gift is from above, and comes down from the Father of lights, with Whom there is no variation or shadow of turning.
JAMES 1:17

Praise the LORD! Praise the LORD, O my soul! While I live I will praise the LORD; I will sing praises to my God while I have my being.
PSALM 146:1–2

I will praise the name of God with a song, and will magnify Him with thanksgiving.
PSALM 69:30

My heart is steadfast, O God, my heart is steadfast; I will sing and give praise. Awake, my glory! Awake, lute and harp! I will awaken the dawn. I will praise You, O Lord, among the peoples; I will sing to You among the nations.
PSALM 57:7–9

Praise the LORD! Oh, give thanks to the LORD, for He is good! For His mercy endures forever. Who can utter the mighty acts of the LORD? Who can declare all His praise?

PSALM 106:1–2

 *THINK THIS:*

In an uncertain world, the one thing I can always depend upon is that God will fulfill His promises for me and my family.

 NOT THAT:

So often I wonder if I can trust God's promises.

I wait for the LORD, my soul waits, and in His word I do hope. My soul waits for the Lord more than those who watch for the morning — yes, more than those who watch for the morning.

PSALM 130:5–6

146

Through the LORD's mercies we are not consumed, because His compassions fail not. They are new every morning; great is Your faithfulness. "The LORD is my portion," says my soul, "therefore I hope in Him!" The LORD is good to those who wait for Him, to the soul who seeks Him.

LAMENTATIONS 3:22–25

The LORD is righteous in her midst, He will do no unrighteousness. Every morning He brings His justice to light; He never fails, but the unjust knows no shame.
ZEPHANIAH 3:5

We are hard-pressed on every side, yet not crushed; we are perplexed, but not in despair; persecuted, but not forsaken; struck down, but not destroyed — always carrying about in the body the dying of the Lord Jesus, that the life of Jesus also may be manifested in our body. For we who live are always delivered to death for Jesus' sake, that the life of Jesus also may be manifested in our mortal flesh.
2 CORINTHIANS 4:8–11

This hope we have as an anchor of the soul, both sure and steadfast, and which enters the Presence behind the veil.
HEBREWS 6:19

For our light affliction, which is but for a moment, is working for us a far more exceeding and eternal weight of glory, while we do not look at the things which are seen, but at the things which are not seen. For the things which are seen are temporary, but the things which are not seen are eternal.
2 CORINTHIANS 4:17–18

For we know that if our earthly house, this tent, is destroyed, we have a building from God, a house not made with hands, eternal in the heavens.
2 CORINTHIANS 5:1

Therefore do not cast away your confidence, which has great reward. For you have need of endurance, so that after you have done the will of God, you may receive the promise.
HEBREWS 10:35–36

I would have lost heart, unless I had believed that I would see the goodness of the LORD in the land of the living. Wait on the LORD; be of good courage, and He shall strengthen your heart; wait, I say, on the LORD!
PSALM 27:13–14

6

MY
FINANCES

THINK THIS:

I trust God to bless me, but my identity and worth are not found in material things.

NOT THAT:

I wish I had more things.

Blessed are those who hunger and thirst for righteousness, for they shall be filled.
MATTHEW 5:6

Not that I speak in regard to need, for I have learned in whatever state I am, to be content: I know how to be abased, and I know how to abound. Everywhere and in all things I have learned both to be full and to be hungry, both to abound and to suffer need. I can do all things through Christ Who strengthens me.
PHILIPPIANS 4:11–13

How precious is Your lovingkindness, O God! Therefore the children of men put their trust under the shadow of Your wings. They are abundantly satisfied with the fullness of Your house, and You give them drink from the river of Your pleasures.
PSALM 36:7–8

Ho! Everyone who thirsts, come to the waters; and you who have no money, come, buy and eat. Yes, come, buy wine and milk without money and without price.
ISAIAH 55:1

The young lions lack and suffer hunger; but those who seek the LORD shall not lack any good thing.

PSALM 34:10

You shall eat in plenty and be satisfied, and praise the name of the LORD your God, Who has dealt wondrously with you: and My people shall never be put to shame.

JOEL 2:26

For He satisfies the longing soul, and fills the hungry soul with goodness.

PSALM 107:9

O God, You are my God; early will I seek You; my soul thirsts for You; my flesh longs for You in a dry and thirsty land where there is no water. So I have looked for You in the sanctuary, to see Your power and Your glory. Because Your lovingkindness is better than life, my lips shall praise You.

PSALM 63:1–3

And God is able to make all grace abound toward you, that you, always having all sufficiency in all things, may have an abundance for every good work.

2 CORINTHIANS 9:8

Bless the LORD, O my soul; and all that is within me, bless His holy name! Bless the LORD, O my soul, and forget not all His benefits: Who forgives all your iniquities, Who heals all your diseases,

Who redeems your life from destruction, Who crowns you with lovingkindness and tender mercies, Who satisfies your mouth with good things, so that your youth is renewed like the eagle's.
PSALM 103:1–5

 **THINK THIS:**

I am equipped for every good work God has planned for me. I am going to see the dreams He has put in my heart come true.

NOT THAT:

I am never going to be successful.

I will instruct you and teach you in the way you should go; I will guide you with My eye.
PSALM 32:8

You did not choose Me, but I chose you and appointed you that you should go and bear fruit, and that your fruit should remain, that whatever you ask the Father in My name He may give you.
JOHN 15:16

I am the vine, you are the branches. He Who abides in Me, and I in him, bears much fruit; for without Me you can do nothing.
JOHN 15:5

But be doers of the word, and not hearers only, deceiving yourselves.
JAMES 1:22

For in Him we live and move and have our being, as also some of your own poets have said, "For we are also His offspring."
ACTS 17:28

I can do all things through Christ Who strengthens me.
PHILIPPIANS 4:13

For I know the thoughts that I think toward you, says the LORD, thoughts of peace and not of evil, to give you a future and a hope.
JEREMIAH 29:11

And keep the charge of the LORD your God: to walk in His ways, to keep His statutes, His commandments, His judgments, and His testimonies, as it is written in the Law of Moses, that you may prosper in all that you do and wherever you turn.
1 KINGS 2:3

 **THINK THIS:**
I am not defined or dependent on my bank account. God is my source, and I look to Him.

 NOT THAT:
My security depends on my financial resources.

He who trusts in his riches will fall, but the righteous will flourish like foliage.
PROVERBS 11:28

Listen, my beloved brethren: Has God not chosen the poor of this world to be rich in faith and heirs of the kingdom which He promised to those who love Him?
JAMES 2:5

Command those who are rich in this present age not to be haughty, nor to trust in uncertain riches but in the living God, Who gives us richly all things to enjoy.
1 TIMOTHY 6:17–19

And my God shall supply all your need according to His riches in glory by Christ Jesus.
PHILIPPIANS 4:19

And when He had fasted forty days and forty nights, afterward He was hungry. Now when the tempter came to Him, he said, "If You are the Son of God, command that these stones become bread."

But He answered and said, "It is written, 'Man shall not live by bread alone, but by every word that proceeds from the mouth of God.'"
MATTHEW 4:2–4

Poverty and shame will come to him who disdains correction, but he who regards a rebuke will be honored.
PROVERBS 13:18

Now godliness with contentment is great gain. For we brought nothing into this world, and it is certain we can carry nothing out. And having food and clothing, with these we shall be content. But those who desire to be rich fall into temptation and a snare, and into many foolish and harmful lusts which drown men in destruction and perdition.
1 TIMOTHY 6:6–9

 **THINK THIS:**
Favor, promotion, and increase are coming my way. God loves me, and He loves to bless me.

 NOT THAT:
My financial circumstance will never improve.

The LORD will grant you plenty of goods, in the fruit of your body, in the increase of your livestock,

and in the produce of your ground, in the land of which the LORD swore to your fathers to give you. The LORD will open to you His good treasure, the heavens, to give the rain to your land in its season, and to bless all the work of your hand. You shall lend to many nations, but you shall not borrow. And the LORD will make you the head and not the tail; you shall be above only, and not be beneath, if you heed the commandments of the LORD your God, which I command you today, and are careful to observe them.
DEUTERONOMY 28:11–13

The LORD is my shepherd; I shall not want.
PSALM 23:1

But this I say: He who sows sparingly will also reap sparingly, and he who sows bountifully will also reap bountifully. So let each one give as he purposes in his heart, not grudgingly or of necessity; for God loves a cheerful giver. And God is able to make all grace abound toward you, that you, always having all sufficiency in all things, may have an abundance for every good work.
2 CORINTHIANS 9:6–8

Remember the LORD your God, for it is He Who gives you power to get wealth, that He may establish His covenant which He swore to your fathers, as it is this day.
DEUTERONOMY 8:18

Beloved, I pray that you may prosper in all things and be in health, just as your soul prospers.
3 JOHN 2

I have been young, and now am old; yet I have not seen the righteous forsaken, nor his descendants begging bread.
PSALM 37:25

Do not lay up for yourselves treasures on earth, where moth and rust destroy and where thieves break in and steal; but lay up for yourselves treasures in heaven, where neither moth nor rust destroys and where thieves do not break in and steal. For where your treasure is, there your heart will be also.
MATTHEW 6:19–21

 *THINK THIS:*

I choose to celebrate the success of others rather than compare myself to them. If God can bless them, I know He can bless me too.

 NOT THAT:

I should be able to have the same things everyone else has.

But those who desire to be rich fall into temptation and a snare, and into many foolish and harmful lusts which drown men in destruction and perdition. For the love of money is a root of all kinds of

evil, for which some have strayed from the faith in their greediness, and pierced themselves through with many sorrows.
1 TIMOTHY 6:9-10

. . . thefts, covetousness, wickedness, deceit, lewdness, an evil eye, blasphemy, pride, foolishness. All these evil things come from within and defile a man.
MARK 7:22-23

. . . having eyes full of adultery and that cannot cease from sin, enticing unstable souls. They have a heart trained in covetous practices, and are accursed children.
2 PETER 2:14

You shall not covet your neighbor's house; you shall not covet your neighbor's wife, nor his male servant, nor his female servant, nor his ox, nor his donkey, nor anything that is your neighbor's.
EXODUS 20:17

He who loves silver will not be satisfied with silver; nor he who loves abundance, with increase. This also is vanity.
ECCLESIASTES 5:10

And He said to them, "Take heed and beware of covetousness, for one's life does not consist in the abundance of the things he possesses."
LUKE 12:15

THINK THIS:

God is my provider and my supply.
I have nothing to worry about
or fear. He will make a way.

NOT THAT:

All I do is worry about finances. I'm not
going to have enough to pay my bills.

The LORD is on my side; I will not fear. What can man do to me? The LORD is for me among those who help me; therefore I shall see my desire on those who hate me. It is better to trust in the LORD than to put confidence in man.
PSALM 118:6–8

You will keep him in perfect peace, whose mind is stayed on You, because he trusts in You. Trust in the LORD forever, for in YAH, the LORD, is everlasting strength.
ISAIAH 26:3–4

It shall come to pass that before they call, I will answer; and while they are still speaking, I will hear.
ISAIAH 65:24

Behold, God is my salvation, I will trust and not be afraid; for YAH, the LORD, is my strength and song; He also has become my salvation.
ISAIAH 12:2

Yes, we had the sentence of death in ourselves, that we should not trust in ourselves but in God Who raises the dead, Who delivered us from so great a death, and does deliver us; in Whom we trust that He will still deliver us.
2 CORINTHIANS 1:9–10

In You, O LORD, I put my trust; let me never be put to shame.
PSALM 71:1

He will not be afraid of evil tidings; his heart is steadfast, trusting in the LORD. His heart is established; he will not be afraid, until he sees his desire upon his enemies.
PSALM 112:7–8

But the salvation of the righteous is from the LORD; He is their strength in the time of trouble. And the LORD shall help them and deliver them; He shall deliver them from the wicked, and save them, because they trust in Him.
PSALM 37:39–40

 *THINK THIS:*

I am blessed to be a blessing to others.

 NOT THAT:

I can't afford to be generous. I have to hang onto everything I get.

But do not forget to do good and to share, for with such sacrifices God is well pleased.
HEBREWS 13:16

So let each one give as he purposes in his heart, not grudgingly or of necessity; for God loves a cheerful giver.
2 CORINTHIANS 9:7

For God is not unjust to forget your work and labor of love which you have shown toward His name, in that you have ministered to the saints, and do minister.
HEBREWS 6:10

For you know the grace of our Lord Jesus Christ, that though He was rich, yet for your sakes He became poor, that you through His poverty might become rich.
2 CORINTHIANS 8:9

Is it not to share your bread with the hungry, and that you bring to your house the poor who are cast out; when you see the naked, that you cover him, and not hide yourself from your own flesh?
ISAIAH 58:7

He has dispersed abroad, He has given to the poor; His righteousness endures forever; His horn will be exalted with honor.
PSALM 112:9

. . . distributing to the needs of the saints, given to hospitality.
ROMANS 12:13

Therefore, as we have opportunity, let us do good to all, especially to those who are of the household of faith.
GALATIANS 6:10

For the poor will never cease from the land; therefore I command you, saying, "You shall open your hand wide to your brother, to your poor and your needy, in your land."
DEUTERONOMY 15:11

I have shown you in every way, by laboring like this, that you must support the weak. And remember the words of the Lord Jesus, that He said, "It is more blessed to give than to receive."
ACTS 20:35

 *THINK THIS:*

God's timing is perfect. He will provide a more-than-enough blessing when the time is right.

 NOT THAT:

I am so tired of waiting for my finances to improve.

Rest in the LORD, and wait patiently for Him; do not fret because of him who prospers in his way, because of the man who brings wicked schemes to pass.
PSALM 37:7

But the ones that fell on the good ground are those who, having heard the word with a noble and good heart, keep it and bear fruit with patience.
LUKE 8:15

By your patience possess your souls.
LUKE 21:19

But also for this very reason, giving all diligence, add to your faith virtue, to virtue knowledge, to knowledge self-control, to self-control perseverance, to perseverance godliness.
2 PETER 1:5–6

My brethren, count it all joy when you fall into various trials, knowing that the testing of your faith produces patience. But let patience have its perfect work, that you may be perfect and complete, lacking nothing.
JAMES 1:2–4

Therefore we also, since we are surrounded by so great a cloud of witnesses, let us lay aside every weight, and the sin which so easily ensnares us, and let us run with endurance the race that is set before us.
HEBREWS 12:1

And let us not grow weary while doing good, for in due season we shall reap if we do not lose heart.
GALATIANS 6:9

It is good that one should hope and wait quietly for the salvation of the LORD. It is good for a man to bear the yoke in his youth.
LAMENTATIONS 3:26–27

But if we hope for what we do not see, we eagerly wait for it with perseverance.
ROMANS 8:25

For whatever things were written before were written for our learning, that we through the patience and comfort of the Scriptures might have hope. Now may the God of patience and comfort grant you to be like-minded toward one another, according to Christ Jesus.
ROMANS 15:4–5

MY FAMILY AND MY MARRIAGE

THINK THIS:

God loves my children, and He has a wonderful plan for their lives. They belong to Him; I have nothing to fear.

NOT THAT:

I'm so worried about my children.

Children are a heritage from the LORD, the fruit of the womb is a reward. Like arrows in the hand of a warrior, so are the children of one's youth. Happy is the man who has his quiver full of them; they shall not be shamed, but shall speak with their enemies in the gate.
PSALM 127:3-5

As for me and my house, we will serve the LORD.
JOSHUA 24:15

And these words which I command you today shall be in your heart. You shall teach them diligently to your children, and shall talk of them when you sit in your house, when you walk by the way, when you lie down, and when you rise up. You shall bind them as a sign on your hand, and they shall be as frontlets between your eyes. You shall write them on the doorposts of your house and on your gates.
DEUTERONOMY 6:6-9

Lift up your eyes all around, and see: they all gather together, they come to you; your sons shall come

from afar, and your daughters shall be nursed at your side.
ISAIAH 60:4

For you shall expand to the right and to the left, and your descendants will inherit the nations, and make the desolate cities inhabited.
ISAIAH 54:3

And he will turn the hearts of the fathers to the children, and the hearts of the children to their fathers, lest I come and strike the earth with a curse.
MALACHI 4:6

Blessed is every one who fears the LORD, who walks in His ways. When you eat the labor of your hands, you shall be happy, and it shall be well with you. Your wife shall be like a fruitful vine in the very heart of your house, your children like olive plants all around your table. Behold, thus shall the man be blessed who fears the LORD.
PSALM 128:1–4

Believe on the Lord Jesus Christ, and you will be saved, you and your household.
ACTS 16:31

Train up a child in the way he should go, and when he is old he will not depart from it.
PROVERBS 22:6

And you, fathers, do not provoke your children to wrath, but bring them up in the training and admonition of the Lord.
EPHESIANS 6:4

 *THINK THIS:*
I am growing stronger, wiser, and healthier. The days ahead of me are greater than the days behind me.

 *NOT THAT:*
I'm worried I won't have enough to take care of my loved ones in my later years.

Those who are planted in the house of the LORD shall flourish in the courts of our God. They shall still bear fruit in old age; they shall be fresh and flourishing, to declare that the LORD is upright; He is my rock, and there is no unrighteousness in Him.
PSALM 92:13–15

With long life I will satisfy him, and show him My salvation.
PSALM 91:16

Surely goodness and mercy shall follow me all the days of my life; and I will dwell in the house of the LORD forever.
PSALM 23:6

O God, You have taught me from my youth; and to this day I declare Your wondrous works. Now also when I am old and grayheaded, O God, do not forsake me, until I declare Your strength to this generation, Your power to everyone who is to come.
PSALM 71:17–18

. . . You shall go to your fathers in peace; you shall be buried at a good old age.
GENESIS 15:15

Now the LORD blessed the latter days of Job more than his beginning . . .
JOB 42:12

For David, after he had served his own generation by the will of God, fell asleep . . .
ACTS 13:36

Yea, though I walk through the valley of the shadow of death, I will fear no evil; for You are with me; Your rod and Your staff, they comfort me.
PSALM 23:4

Even to your old age, I am He, and even to gray hairs I will carry you! I have made, and I will bear; even I will carry, and will deliver you.
ISAIAH 46:4

Let your heart keep my commands; for length of days and long life and peace they will add to you.
PROVERBS 3:1–2

I have been young, and now am old; yet I have not seen the righteous forsaken, nor his descendants begging bread.
PSALM 37:25

 *THINK THIS:*

My family is blessed, anointed, favored, chosen and loved by God. His blessings are chasing us down.

 NOT THAT:

It doesn't feel like my family is blessed.

And if it seems evil to you to serve the LORD, choose for yourselves this day whom you will serve, whether the gods which your fathers served that were on the other side of the River, or the gods of the Amorites, in whose land you dwell. But as for me and my house, we will serve the LORD.
JOSHUA 24:15

. . . one who rules his own house well, having his children in submission with all reverence (for if a man does not know how to rule his own house, how will he take care of the church of God?) . . .
1 TIMOTHY 3:4–5

Your wife shall be like a fruitful vine in the very heart of your house, your children like olive plants all around your table. Behold, thus shall the man be blessed who fears the LORD. The LORD bless you out of Zion, and may you see the good of Jerusalem all the days of your life. Yes, may you see your children's children. Peace be upon Israel!

PSALM 128:3–6

And these words which I command you today shall be in your heart. You shall teach them diligently to your children, and shall talk of them when you sit in your house, when you walk by the way, when you lie down, and when you rise up. You shall bind them as a sign on your hand, and they shall be as front-lets between your eyes. You shall write them on the doorposts of your house and on your gates.

DEUTERONOMY 6:6–9

She watches over the ways of her household, and does not eat the bread of idleness. Her children rise up and call her blessed; her husband also, and he praises her.

PROVERBS 31:27–28

Behold, how good and how pleasant it is for brethren to dwell together in unity!

PSALM 133:1

For I have known him, in order that he may command his children and his household after him, that they keep the way of the LORD, to do righteousness and justice, that the LORD may bring to Abraham what He has spoken to him.

GENESIS 18:19

I call to remembrance the genuine faith that is in you, which dwelt first in your grandmother Lois and your mother Eunice, and I am persuaded is in you also.
2 TIMOTHY 1:5

 **THINK THIS:**

God sees my sorrow, and He is binding up my broken heart. Joy is returning to my life.

 NOT THAT:

I miss my loved one; I am so lonely.

Therefore you now have sorrow; but I will see you again and your heart will rejoice, and your joy no one will take from you.
JOHN 16:22

I will betroth you to Me forever; yes, I will betroth you to Me in righteousness and justice, in loving-kindness and mercy; I will betroth you to Me in faithfulness, and you shall know the LORD.
HOSEA 2:19–20

I caused the widow's heart to sing for joy.
JOB 29:13

You have turned for me my mourning into dancing; You have put off my sackcloth and clothed me with gladness.
PSALM 30:11

A father of the fatherless, a defender of the widows, is God in His holy habitation.
PSALM 68:5

He administers justice for the fatherless and the widow, and loves the stranger, giving him food and clothing.
DEUTERONOMY 10:18

Pure and undefiled religion before God and the Father is this: to visit orphans and widows in their trouble, and to keep oneself unspotted from the world.
JAMES 1:27

The LORD watches over the strangers; He relieves the fatherless and widow; but the way of the wicked He turns upside down.
PSALM 146:9

Do not fear, for you will not be ashamed; neither be disgraced, for you will not be put to shame; for you will forget the shame of your youth, and will not remember the reproach of your widowhood anymore. For your Maker is your husband, the LORD of hosts is His name; and your Redeemer is the Holy One of Israel; He is called the God of the whole earth.
ISAIAH 54:4–5

I am the head, not the tail — above, not beneath. God's plan for my life isn't dependent on what others think or say about me.

NOT THAT:

My own family rejects me. How can I be worth anything?

I will make you an eternal excellence, a joy of many generations.
ISAIAH 60:15

(For the LORD your God is a merciful God), He will not forsake you nor destroy you, nor forget the covenant of your fathers which He swore to them.
DEUTERONOMY 4:31

It is better to trust in the LORD than to put confidence in man.
PSALM 118:8

Can a woman forget her nursing child, and not have compassion on the son of her womb? Surely they may forget, yet I will not forget you. See, I have inscribed you on the palms of My hands; your walls are continually before Me.
ISAIAH 49:15&16

Be strong, and of good courage, do not fear nor be afraid of them; for the LORD your God, He is the

One Who goes with you. He will not leave you nor forsake you.
DEUTERONOMY 31:6

"Surely your salvation is coming; behold, His reward is with Him, and His work before Him." And they shall call them The Holy People, the Redeemed of the LORD; and you shall be called Sought Out, a City Not Forsaken.
ISAIAH 62:11–12

For the LORD will not forsake His people, for His great name's sake, because it has pleased the LORD to make you His people.
1 SAMUEL 12:22

And those who know Your name will trust in You; for You, LORD, have not forsaken those who seek You.
PSALM 9:10

When my father and my mother forsake me, then the LORD will take care of me.
PSALM 27:10

You are God, ready to pardon, gracious and merciful, slow to anger, abundant in kindness, and did not forsake them.
NEHEMIAH 9:17

You shall no longer be termed Forsaken, nor shall your land any more be termed Desolate; but you shall be called Hephzibah, and your land Beulah;

for the LORD delights in you, and your land shall be married.
ISAIAH 62:4

For the LORD will not cast off His people, nor will He forsake His inheritance.
PSALM 94:14

I have been young, and now am old; yet I have not seen the righteous forsaken, nor his descendants begging bread. He is ever merciful, and lends; and his descendants are blessed.
PSALM 37:25–26

 THINK THIS:

God is fighting for my family. This situation is not a surprise to Him. He will work every detail to our advantage.

 NOT THAT:

It feels like my family is in a battle that we're losing.

And the LORD will deliver me from every evil work and preserve me for His heavenly kingdom. To Him be glory forever and ever. Amen!
2 TIMOTHY 4:18

And he said: "The LORD is my rock and my fortress and my deliverer; the God of my strength, in Whom

I will trust; my shield and the horn of my salvation, my stronghold and my refuge; my Savior, You save me from violence."
2 SAMUEL 22:2–3

I will say of the LORD, "He is my refuge and my fortress; my God, in Him I will trust." Surely He shall deliver you from the snare of the fowler and from the perilous pestilence.
PSALM 91:2–3

You are of God, little children, and have overcome them, because He Who is in you is greater than he who is in the world.
1 JOHN 4:4

And they overcame him by the blood of the Lamb and by the word of their testimony, and they did not love their lives to the death.
REVELATION 12:11

And you shall know the truth, and the truth shall make you free.
JOHN 8:32

Then the seventy returned with joy, saying, "Lord, even the demons are subject to us in Your name."
LUKE 10:17

You are my hiding place; You shall preserve me from trouble; You shall surround me with songs of deliverance.
PSALM 32:7

The Spirit of the LORD is upon Me, because He has anointed Me to preach the gospel to the poor; He has sent Me to heal the brokenhearted, to proclaim liberty to the captives and recovery of sight to the blind, to set at liberty those who are oppressed; to proclaim the acceptable year of the LORD.
LUKE 4:18–19

For the law of the Spirit of life in Christ Jesus has made me free from the law of sin and death.
ROMANS 8:2

But now having been set free from sin, and having become slaves of God, you have your fruit to holiness, and the end, everlasting life.
ROMAN 6:22

And do not lead us into temptation, but deliver us from the evil one. For Yours is the kingdom and the power and the glory forever. Amen.
MATTHEW 6:13

 **THINK THIS:**

My family will be different. God is bringing
us together. He is redeeming lost time. He
is establishing generational blessings.

 NOT THAT:

So many families are crumbling,
and I'm afraid mine will be next.

Be strong and of good courage, do not fear nor be
afraid of them; for the LORD your God, He is the
One Who goes with you. He will not leave you nor
forsake you.
DEUTERONOMY 31:6

So he answered and said to me: "This is the word
of the LORD to Zerubbabel: Not by might nor by
power, but by My Spirit," says the LORD of hosts.
ZECHARIAH 4:6

In the day when I cried out, You answered me, and
made me bold with strength in my soul.
PSALM 138:3

For the LORD will be your confidence, and will keep
your foot from being caught.
PROVERBS 3:26

For I am not ashamed of the gospel of Christ,
for it is the power of God to salvation for everyone who believes, for the Jew first and also for the

Greek. For in it the righteousness of God is revealed from faith to faith; as it is written, "The just shall live by faith."
ROMANS 1:16–17

Most assuredly, I say to you, he who believes in Me, the works that I do he will do also; and greater works than these he will do, because I go to My Father.
JOHN 14:12

So we may boldly say: "The LORD is my helper; I will not fear. What can man do to me?"
HEBREWS 13:6

The LORD God is my strength; He will make my feet like deer's feet, and He will make me walk on my high hills.
HABAKKUK 3:19

Now this is the confidence that we have in Him, that if we ask anything according to His will, He hears us. And if we know that He hears us, whatever we ask, we know that we have the petitions that we have asked of Him.
1 JOHN 5:14–15

I can do all things through Christ Who strengthens me.
PHILIPPIANS 4:13

Now He Who searches the hearts knows what the mind of the Spirit is, because He makes intercession for the saints according to the will of God.

ROMANS 8:27

. . . being confident of this very thing, that He Who has begun a good work in you will complete it until the day of Jesus Christ.

PHILIPPIANS 1:6

Therefore do not cast away your confidence, which has great reward. For you have need of endurance, so that after you have done the will of God, you may receive the promise.

HEBREWS 10:35–36

 *THINK THIS:*

God is chasing my loved ones down with His goodness and mercy. The end of their story hasn't been written yet. God can do the seemingly impossible.

 NOT THAT:

My loved one who is off track will never come back to God.

For the Son of Man has come to seek and to save that which was lost.

LUKE 19:10

The Lord is not slack concerning His promises, as some count slackness, but is longsuffering toward us, not willing that any should perish but that all should come to repentance.
2 PETER 3:9

Restore to me the joy of Your salvation, and uphold me by Your generous Spirit. Then I will teach transgressors Your ways, and sinners shall be converted to You.
PSALM 51:12–13

God did not send His Son into the world to condemn the world, but that the world through Him might be saved.
JOHN 3:17

There will be more joy in heaven over one sinner who repents than over ninety-nine just persons who need no repentance.
LUKE 15:7

But when he was still a great way off, his father saw him and had compassion, and ran and fell on his neck and kissed him. And the son said to him, "Father, I have sinned against heaven and in your sight, and am no longer worthy to be called your son." But the father said to his servants, "Bring out the best robe and put it on him, and put a ring on his hand and sandals on his feet. And bring the fatted calf here and kill it, and let us eat and be merry; for this my son was dead and is alive again; he was lost and is found." And they began to be merry.

LUKE 15:20–24

So they said, "Believe on the Lord Jesus Christ, and you will be saved, you and your household." Then they spoke the word of the Lord to him and to all who were in his house. And he took them the same hour of the night and washed their stripes. And immediately he and all his family were baptized. Now when he had brought them into his house, he set food before them; and he rejoiced, having believed in God with all his household.

ACTS 16:31–34

Those who sow in tears shall reap in joy. He who continually goes forth weeping, bearing seed for sowing, shall doubtless come again with rejoicing, bringing his sheaves with him.

PSALM 126:5–6

Come to Me, all you who labor and are heavy laden, and I will give you rest. Take My yoke upon you and learn from Me, for I am gentle and lowly in heart, and you will find rest for your souls. For My yoke is easy and My burden is light.

MATTHEW 11:28–30

THINK THIS:
I know God's dream for me and my family is coming to pass. I am not alone; He is with me. He will establish His perfect plan for us.

NOT THAT:
I don't know what to do, and I don't know where to turn for help.

I will meditate on Your precepts, and contemplate Your ways. I will delight myself in Your statutes; I will not forget Your word.
PSALM 119:15–16

So then faith comes by hearing, and hearing by the word of God.
ROMANS 10:17

Evening and morning and at noon I will pray, and cry aloud, and He shall hear my voice.
PSALM 55:17

The LORD is far from the wicked, but He hears the prayer of the righteous.
PROVERBS 15:29

Now when Daniel knew that the writing was signed, he went home. And in his upper room, with his windows open toward Jerusalem, he knelt down on his knees three times that day, and

prayed and gave thanks before his God, as was his custom since early days.
DANIEL 6:10

But these are the ones sown on good ground, those who hear the word, accept it, and bear fruit: some thirtyfold, some sixty, and some a hundred.
MARK 4:20

Your word is a lamp to my feet and a light to my path.
PSALM 119:105

A man's heart plans his way, but the LORD directs his steps.
PROVERBS 16:9

The lot is cast into the lap, but its every decision is from the LORD.
PROVERBS 16:33

 *THINK THIS:*

I am not a victim; I am a victor. I will not live in the pain of the past. I choose to trust God and believe the best is yet to come.

 NOT THAT:

A loved one has broken my heart, and I can't trust anymore.

The LORD is near to those who have a broken heart, and saves such as have a contrite spirit. Many are the afflictions of the righteous, but the LORD delivers him out of them all.

PSALM 34:18–19

The LORD also will be a refuge for the oppressed, a refuge in times of trouble. And those who know Your name will put their trust in You; for You, LORD, have not forsaken those who seek You.

PSALM 9:9–10

In the day when I cried out, You answered me, and made me bold with strength in my soul.

PSALM 138:3

Come to Me, all you who labor and are heavy laden, and I will give you rest. Take My yoke upon you and learn from Me, for I am gentle and lowly in heart, and you will find rest for your souls.

MATTHEW 11:28–29

The LORD will guide you continually, and satisfy your soul in drought, and strengthen your bones; you shall be like a watered garden, and like a spring of water, whose waters do not fail.

ISAIAH 58:11

He heals the brokenhearted and binds up their wounds.

PSALM 147:3

 **THINK THIS:**

God has blessed my family abundantly.
His grace covers over our weaknesses.
He is the source of every good thing.

 NOT THAT:

My family really has it together;
people could learn a lot from us.

My soul shall make its boast in the LORD; the humble shall hear of it and be glad.
PSALM 34:2

He has shown you, O man, what is good; and what does the LORD require of you but to do justly, to love mercy, and to walk humbly with your God?
MICAH 6:8

Let this mind be in you which was also in Christ Jesus, Who, being in the form of God, did not consider it robbery to be equal with God, but made Himself of no reputation, taking the form of a bondservant, and coming in the likeness of men. And being found in appearance as a man, He humbled Himself and became obedient to the point of death, even the death of the cross.
PHILIPPIANS 2:5–8

"For all those things My hand has made, and all those things exist," says the LORD. "But on this one will I look: On him who is poor and of a contrite spirit, and who trembles at My word."
ISAIAH 66:2

Though the LORD is on high, yet He regards the lowly; but the proud He knows from afar.
PSALM 138:6

Then He will save the humble person.
JOB 22:29

For whoever exalts himself will be humbled, and he who humbles himself will be exalted.
LUKE 14:11

But He gives more grace. Therefore He says: "God resists the proud, but gives grace to the humble."
JAMES 4:6

Before destruction the heart of a man is haughty, and before honor is humility.
PROVERBS 18:12

By humility and the fear of the LORD are riches and honor and life.
PROVERBS 22:4

Therefore, as the elect of God, holy and beloved, put on tender mercies, kindness, humility, meekness, longsuffering.
COLOSSIANS 3:12

THINK THIS:

I refuse to be held back by bitterness and unforgiveness. Instead, I choose to forgive and receive God's healing for my soul.

NOT THAT:

I can never forgive what was done to me.

But if you do not forgive men their trespasses, neither will your Father forgive your trespasses.
MATTHEW 6:14-15

. . . bearing with one another, and forgiving one another, if anyone has a complaint against another; even as Christ forgave you, so you also must do.
COLOSSIANS 3:13

Now may the God of patience and comfort grant you to be like-minded toward one another, according to Christ Jesus, that you may with one mind and one mouth glorify the God and Father of our Lord Jesus Christ. Therefore receive one another, just as Christ also received us, to the glory of God.
ROMANS 15:5-7

. . . not returning evil for evil or reviling for reviling, but on the contrary blessing, knowing that you were called to this, that you may inherit a blessing.
1 PETER 3:9

And forgive us our sins, for we also forgive everyone who is indebted to us.
LUKE 11:4

Take heed to yourselves. If your brother sins against you, rebuke him; and if he repents, forgive him.
LUKE 17:3

And whenever you stand praying, if you have anything against anyone, forgive him, that your Father in heaven may also forgive you your trespasses.
MARK 11:25

Do not remember the former things, nor consider the things of old.
ISAIAH 43:18

Who when He was reviled, did not revile in return; when He suffered, He did not threaten, but committed Himself to Him who judges righteously.
1 PETER 2:23

Let all bitterness, wrath, anger, clamor, and evil speaking be put away from you, with all malice. And be kind to one another, tenderhearted, forgiving one another, even as God in Christ forgave you.
EPHESIANS 4:31–32

Love your enemies, bless those who curse you, do good to those who hate you, and pray for those who spitefully use you and persecute you.
MATTHEW 5:44

Then Peter came to Him and said, 'Lord, how often shall my brother sin against me, and I forgive him? Up to seven times?' Jesus said to him, 'I do not say to you, up to seven times, but up to seventy times seven.'

MATTHEW 18:21–22

 *THINK THIS:*

God has solutions already lined up. He can redeem the lost time. My marriage can be healed and stronger than ever.

 *NOT THAT:*

My marriage is falling apart, and I don't see how we can make it.

Love suffers long and is kind; love does not envy; love does not parade itself, is not puffed up; does not behave rudely, does not seek its own, is not provoked, thinks no evil; does not rejoice in iniquity, but rejoices in the truth; bears all things, believes all things, hopes all things, endures all things. Love never fails.

1 CORINTHIANS 13:4–8

Therefore a man shall leave his father and mother and be joined to his wife, and they shall become one flesh.

GENESIS 2:24

Finally, all of you be of one mind, having compassion for one another; love as brothers, be tenderhearted, be courteous; not returning evil for evil or reviling for reviling, but on the contrary blessing, knowing that you were called to this, that you may inherit a blessing.
1 PETER 3:8–9

Let each man have his own wife, and let each woman have her own husband. Let the husband render to his wife the affection due her, and likewise also the wife to her husband.
1 CORINTHIANS 7:2–3

Let all bitterness, wrath, anger, clamor, and evil speaking be put away from you, with all malice. And be kind to one another, tenderhearted, forgiving one another, even as God in Christ forgave you.
EPHESIANS 4:31–32

Husbands, love your wives, just as Christ also loved the church and gave Himself for her, that He might sanctify and cleanse her with the washing of water by the word, that He might present her to Himself a glorious church, not having spot or wrinkle or any such thing, but that she should be holy and without blemish. So husbands ought to love their own wives as their own bodies; he who loves his wife loves himself.
EPHESIANS 5:25–28

And the LORD God said, "It is not good that man should be alone; I will make him a helper comparable to him."
GENESIS 2:18

 **THINK THIS:**

Good breaks, the right connections, strength, health, favor, opportunities — I'm standing in faith that I will see God's blessings for me and my family.

 NOT THAT:

I live in constant fear that something bad will happen to my family.

And let the peace of God rule in your hearts, to which also you were called in one body; and be thankful.
COLOSSIANS 3:15

There remains therefore a rest for the people of God.
HEBREWS 4:9

He who dwells in the secret place of the Most High shall abide under the shadow of the Almighty. I will say of the LORD, "He is my refuge and my fortress; my God, in Him I will trust."
PSALM 91:1–2

You will keep him in perfect peace, whose mind is stayed on You, because he trusts in You.
ISAIAH 26:3

Be anxious for nothing, but in everything by prayer and supplication, with thanksgiving, let your requests be made known to God; and the peace of God, which surpasses all understanding, will guard your hearts and minds through Christ Jesus.
PHILIPPIANS 4:6–7

Consider the lilies of the field, how they grow: they neither toil nor spin; and yet I say to you that even Solomon in all his glory was not arrayed like one of these. Now if God so clothes the grass of the field, which today is, and tomorrow is thrown into the oven, will He not much more clothe you, O you of little faith? "Therefore do not worry, saying, 'What shall we eat?' or 'What shall we drink?' or 'What shall we wear?' For after all these things the Gentiles seek. For your heavenly Father knows that you need all these things. But seek first the kingdom of God and His righteousness, and all these things shall be added to you. Therefore do not worry about tomorrow, for tomorrow will worry about its own things. Sufficient for the day is its own trouble."
MATTHEW 6:28–34

I will both lie down in peace, and sleep; for You alone, O LORD, make me dwell in safety.
PSALM 4:8

And my God shall supply all your need according to His riches in glory by Christ Jesus.
PHILIPPIANS 4:19

. . . casting all your care upon Him, for He cares for you.
1 PETER 5:7

 **THINK THIS:**

God is healing me from this hurt and preparing me for a future that is better than I could have imagined.

 NOT THAT:

My divorce has destroyed my life.

For He Himself has said, "I will never leave you nor forsake you." So we may boldly say, "The LORD is my helper; I will not fear. What can man do to me?"
HEBREWS 13:5–6

Yet in all these things we are more than conquerors through Him Who loved us.
ROMANS 8:37

The LORD is near to those who have a broken heart . . .
PSALM 34:18

Do not cast away your confidence, which has great reward.
HEBREWS 10:35

Fear not, for I am with you; be not dismayed, for I am your God. I will strengthen you, yes, I will help you, I will uphold you with My righteous right hand.
ISAIAH 41:10

For the LORD will be your confidence, and will keep your foot from being caught.
PROVERBS 3:26

Blessed be the God and Father of our Lord Jesus Christ, the Father of mercies and God of all comfort, Who comforts us in all our tribulation, that we may be able to comfort those who are in any trouble, with the comfort with which we ourselves are comforted by God.
2 CORINTHIANS 1:3–4

So the ransomed of the LORD shall return, and come to Zion with singing, with everlasting joy on their heads. They shall obtain joy and gladness; sorrow and sighing shall flee away.
ISAIAH 51:11

The Spirit of the Lord GOD is upon Me, because the LORD has anointed Me to preach good tidings to the poor; He has sent Me to heal the brokenhearted, to proclaim liberty to the captives, and the opening of the prison to those who are bound; to proclaim

the acceptable year of the LORD, and the day of vengeance of our God; to comfort all who mourn, to console those who mourn in Zion, to give them beauty for ashes, the oil of joy for mourning, the garment of praise for the spirit of heaviness; that they may be called trees of righteousness, the planting of the LORD, that He may be glorified.
ISAIAH 61:1–3

The LORD God is my strength; He will make my feet like deer's feet, and He will make me walk on my high hills.
HABAKKUK 3:19

 **THINK THIS:**

I know that God has the right person
lined up for me. The dream He has
placed in my heart will come to pass.

 NOT THAT:

I'm so tired of being single;
I'm never going to get married.

Delight yourself also in the LORD, and He shall give you the desires of your heart.
PSALM 37:4

But as God has distributed to each one, as the Lord has called each one, so let him walk.
1 CORINTHIANS 7:17

I will betroth you to Me forever; yes, I will betroth you to Me in righteousness and justice, in loving-kindness and mercy.
HOSEA 2:19

Now this is the confidence that we have in Him, that if we ask anything according to His will, He hears us.
1 JOHN 5:14

Ask, and it will be given to you; seek, and you will find; knock, and it will be opened to you.
MATTHEW 7:7

Most assuredly, I say to you, whatever you ask the Father in My name He will give you.
JOHN 16:23

Now may the God of hope fill you with all joy and peace in believing, that you may abound in hope by the power of the Holy Spirit.
ROMANS 15:13

THINK THIS:

I am going to use my words to bless those around me. I will speak favor and victory over my family, friends, and loved ones. I will call out the seeds of greatness inside of them.

NOT THAT:

I know my words are hurtful, but they're my family; I can say what I want to them.

A wholesome tongue is a tree of life, but perverseness in it breaks the spirit.
PROVERBS 15:4

Whoever guards his mouth and tongue keeps his soul from troubles.
PROVERBS 21:23

Do not be a witness against your neighbor without cause, for would you deceive with your lips?
PROVERBS 24:28

For "He who would love life and see good days, let him refrain his tongue from evil, and his lips from speaking deceit."
1 PETER 3:10

Whoever offers praise glorifies Me; and to him who orders his conduct aright I will show the salvation of God.
PSALM 50:23

Let no corrupt word proceed out of your mouth, but what is good for necessary edification, that it may impart grace to the hearers.
EPHESIANS 4:29

If anyone among you thinks he is religious, and does not bridle his tongue but deceives his own heart, this one's religion is useless.
JAMES 1:26

As long as my breath is in me, and the breath of God in my nostrils, my lips will not speak wickedness, nor my tongue utter deceit.
JOB 27:3–4

 THINK THIS:
I am equipped and empowered to do all that God has called me to do. God knows my heart, and He can turn even my mistakes around for good.

 NOT THAT:
I'm afraid I'm going to make mistakes and be a bad influence for my family.

The righteous man walks in his integrity; his children are blessed after him.
PROVERBS 20:7

If I have walked with falsehood, or if my foot has hastened to deceit, let me be weighed on honest scales, that God may know my integrity.
JOB 31:5–6

The LORD shall judge the peoples; judge me, O LORD, according to my righteousness, and according to my integrity within me.
PSALM 7:8

A good man deals graciously and lends; he will guide his affairs with discretion. Surely he will never be shaken; the righteous will be in everlasting remembrance. He will not be afraid of evil tidings; his heart is steadfast, trusting in the LORD.
PSALM 112:5–7

Blessed is the man who walks not in the counsel of the ungodly, nor stands in the path of sinners, nor sits in the seat of the scornful; but his delight is in the law of the LORD, and in His law he meditates day and night. He shall be like a tree planted by the rivers of water, that brings forth its fruit in its season, whose leaf also shall not wither; and whatever he does shall prosper. The ungodly are not so, but are like the chaff which the wind drives away. Therefore the ungodly shall not stand in the judgment, nor sinners in the congregation of the righteous. For the LORD knows the way of the righteous, but the way of the ungodly shall perish.

PSALM 1:1–6

Far be it from me that I should say you are right; till I die I will not put away my integrity from me. My righteousness I hold fast, and will not let it go; my heart shall not reproach me as long as I live.

JOB 27:5–6

THINK THIS:

God hears the prayers I pray for my family. I'm taking the lid off my prayers and praying bigger prayers than ever for those I love.

NOT THAT:

Does it even matter if I pray for my family?

. . . praying always with all prayer and supplication in the Spirit, being watchful to this end with all perseverance and supplication for all the saints.

EPHESIANS 6:18

Moreover, as for me, far be it from me that I should sin against the LORD in ceasing to pray for you; but I will teach you the good and the right way.

1 SAMUEL 12:23

And behold, a woman of Canaan came from that region and cried out to Him, saying, "Have mercy on me, O Lord, Son of David! My daughter is severely demon-possessed."
MATTHEW 15:22

Therefore I exhort first of all that supplications, prayers, intercessions, and giving of thanks be made for all men.
1 TIMOTHY 2:1

Now therefore, take for yourselves seven bulls and seven rams, go to My servant Job, and offer up for yourselves a burnt offering; and My servant Job shall pray for you. For I will accept him, lest I deal with you according to your folly; because you have not spoken of Me what is right, as My servant Job has.
JOB 42:8

Pray for us; for we are confident that we have a good conscience, in all things desiring to live honorably.
HEBREWS 13:18

Is anyone among you sick? Let him call for the elders of the church, and let them pray over him, anointing him with oil in the name of the Lord. And the prayer of faith will save the sick, and the Lord will raise him up. And if he has committed sins, he will be forgiven. Confess your trespasses to one another, and pray for one another, that you may be

healed. The effective, fervent prayer of a righteous man avails much.
JAMES 5:14–16

And Abraham said to God, "Oh, that Ishmael might live before You!"
GENESIS 17:18

 THINK THIS:
I am going to be a peacemaker in my home. I choose joy, peace, and laughter over anger, negativity, and arguments.

 NOT THAT:
We fight constantly; my family is always arguing. That's just how we are.

Let nothing be done through selfish ambition or conceit, but in lowliness of mind let each esteem others better than himself.
PHILIPPIANS 2:3

A wrathful man stirs up strife, but he who is slow to anger allays contention.
PROVERBS 15:18

The beginning of strife is like releasing water; therefore stop contention before a quarrel starts.
PROVERBS 17:14

Do not strive with a man without cause, if he has done you no harm.
PROVERBS 3:30

For I fear lest, when I come, I shall not find you such as I wish, and that I shall be found by you such as you do not wish; lest there be contentions, jealousies, outbursts of wrath, selfish ambitions, backbitings, whisperings, conceits, tumults.
2 CORINTHIANS 12:20

But if you have bitter envy and self-seeking in your hearts, do not boast and lie against the truth.
JAMES 3:14

. . . endeavoring to keep the unity of the Spirit in the bond of peace.
EPHESIANS 4:3

Now I plead with you, brethren, by the name of our Lord Jesus Christ, that you all speak the same thing, and that there be no divisions among you, but that you be perfectly joined together in the same mind and in the same judgment. For it has been declared to me concerning you, my brethren, by those of Chloe's household, that there are contentions among you.
1 CORINTHIANS 1:10–11